INTERNATIONAL SOCIALISM

A quarterly journal of socialist theory

Winter 1996

Contents

Issue 73 of INTERNATIONAL SOCIALISM, quarterly journal of the Socialist Workers Party (Britain)

Published December 1996
Copyright © International Socialism
Distribution/subscriptions: International Socialism,
PO Box 82, London E3
American distribution: B de Boer, 113 East Center St, Nutley,
New Jersey 07110
Subscriptions and back copies: PO Box 16085, Chicago,
Illinois 60616
Editorial and production: 0171 538 1626/0171 538 0538
Sales and subscriptions: 0171 538 5821
American sales: 312 665 7337

ISBN 1 898876 21 5

Printed by BPC Wheatons Ltd, Exeter, England
Typeset by East End Offset, London E3

Cover illustration by Tim Sanders, design by Sherborne Design

For details of back copies see the end pages of this book

Subscription rates for one year (four issues) are:

Britain and overseas (surface):	individual	£14 ($30)
	institutional	£25
Air speeded supplement:	North America	nil
	Europe/South America	£2
	elsewhere	£4

Note to contributors

The deadline for articles intended for issue 76 of *International Socialism* is 1 February 1997.

All contributions should be double spaced with wide margins. Please submit two copies. If you write your contribution using a computer, please also supply a disk, together with details of the computer and programme used.

INTERNATIONAL SOCIALISM ★

A quarterly journal of socialist theory

'GLOBALISATION' HAS become the new orthodoxy of establishment economics—as much for the supporters of Tony Blair's New Labour as for free market conservatives. Chris Harman examines the claim that the world market is now such a powerful force that neither states nor organised labour can withstand its pressures. He debunks the assertions of globalisation theorists and gives a careful account of the inter-relationship between multinational capital, the state and the modern working class.

SPORT IS played and watched by millions of working class people—and big business makes millions out of them as they do so. Chris Bambery looks at the links between capitalism and sport, at why people enjoy sport and at the argument that physical recreation and the modern form of sport are by no means the same thing.

A DEBATE about materialism, evolution and intelligence has been sparked by Alex Callinicos's review of Daniel Dennett's *Darwin's Dangerous Idea* in issue 71 of *International Socialism*. John Parrington and Joe Faith put forward their positions in this issue.

AMERICA'S REVOLUTION is the subject of Megan Trudell's critique of Theodore Draper's controversial *The Struggle for Power*. She looks at Draper's materialist account and the objections raised against it by Draper's critics. Other reviews include Mark O'Brien's look at the first three books in the 'Socialist History of Britain' series produced under the direction of the Northern Marxist Historians group.

THE FIRST of our new *Review article* feature, which will alternate with our established *Bookwatch* series, is Charlie Kimber's timely examination of the descent into barbarism in Rwanda and Burundi.

Editor: John Rees. Assistant Editors: Alex Callinicos, Chris Harman, John Molyneux, Lindsey German, Colin Sparks, Mike Gonzalez, Peter Morgan, Gill Hubbard, Mike Haynes, Judy Cox, Adrian Budd, Ian Goodyer, Mark O'Brien and Rob Hoveman.

Globalisation: a critique of a new orthodoxy

CHRIS HARMAN

'Globalisation' has become one of the orthodoxies of the 1990s. The word dots financial pages and company reports, is heard in the speeches of virtually all mainstream politicians, from John Redwood to Tony Blair, is common currency in corporation newsletters and shop stewards meetings. Everywhere it is used to mean that the world economy has reached a new stage, which governments and workers alike are virtually powerless to withstand.

This new stage is supposed to have been brought about by a growing internationalisation of production and marketing. Companies, it is said, are much more dependent than ever before on their ability to sell abroad in the face of 'global competition'. They can only do this successfully insofar as they become multinational corporations, organising production itself on an international scale, ignoring national borders. They are then able to escape any control by national states or by workers' movements that operate within national boundaries. They are free to move their capital to wherever labour is cheapest, thus thwarting workers' attempts to defend wages and conditions through trade union action.

This consensus is usually articulated by 'neo-liberal' proponents of free market capitalism. They insist that the new global order rules out any attempt to regulate the system through Keynesianism or state capitalism, let alone socialism. Any such attempt, they claim, can only result in a backward siege economy, indeed, in a horrific repeat of Cambodia's year zero. But it is not only far reaching change which is ruled out. So are the mildest reforms—a minimum wage of more than about a third of the median, any further reduction of the working week, any attempt to protect jobs against the withering effects of recession. If workers push their demands too hard, then companies will simply pack up their bags and move elsewhere. If governments implement meaningful reforms, then new investment will simply flow to more profitable parts of the world. All that can be done is to elaborate policies which will make any particular group of workers more productive and cost efficient than those elsewhere in the world, or which enable one government to outbid others in guaranteeing profitability.

These claims underpin the explanations provided by mainstream 'neo-classical' economists for the increasing gap, in virtually every country, between the incomes of the rich and those of the mass of people. The wealthy, it is claimed, are 'rewarded' for having skills which are in short supply, while the workers are paying the price of for having skills which are easily replaced through the world labour market. But the argument about 'globalisation' has a wider resonance. It is echoed both by some on the revolutionary left and some of the protectionist far right. Thus one former editor of this journal, Nigel Harris, wrote more than a decade ago of:

> *...a single global labour market, moving towards one price for labour for each skill grade regardless of whether the countries are more or less developed... This implies that groups of workers in different countries compete with each other for employment, offering employers the lowest price at a given level of labour productivity. The power of trade unions to influence this bargain...in the international context hardly exists at all.*[1]

More recently James Goldsmith, the billionaire right wing scourge of the Tory party, claimed in an interview in *Tribune*:

> *Something created unemployment. It was not high technology, which is the usual excuse. What you have is the mass movement of manufacturing offshore... The system pays the owners of a company to close factories, put everyone out of work and move it offshore. And this is happening across the spectrum. It covers manufacturing and services... Transnational corporations today are few in number, but move at great speed to wherever labour is cheapest.*[2]

So powerful has this consensus about 'globalisation' become that those who still want to challenge the logic of the world system are often treated as throwbacks to the past. This is a particularly anomalous situation for revolutionary socialists to do be in, since it was not so long ago that we were dismissed out of hand by much of mainstream thought for our stress on the power of international capitalism.

However, there are a few voices outside the revolutionary left who are prepared to say that the king has few clothes. The radical American economist David Gordon challenged the consensus in an important article eight years ago. More recently the academic reformists Paul Hirst and Grahame Thompson, the influential non-Marxist sociologist Michael Mann, and W Ruigrok and R van Tulder have challenged the globalisation thesis frontally.[3] Most of their practical conclusions are very different from ours: Mann, Hirst and Thompson in particular want to find space for old style reformism, marshalling arguments which Hirst, for instance, was already using in a debate with Alex Callinicos 18 years ago.[4] Yet their challenges to the consensus are worth examining seriously, because they do punch holes in some of its major contentions, even if they are absolutely confused as what to put in its place.

The counter-argument

The core of their argument is that 'globalisation' orthodoxy may start with a few incontestable facts, but some these are not even new. And the orthodoxy proceeds to erect on them an account of the world economy and of the behaviour of firms within it which differs in many important respects from reality. All too often its adherents confuse what 'neo-classical' free market economic theory says *ought* to be the case with what *actually* happens.

There is nothing new about the international character of capitalism. The search for markets as far across the world as possible and the movement of funds across state boundaries have been a characteristic of capitalism from its origins in the middle ages.[5] The classical political economist Ricardo was insisting as far back as 1821 that the state should not try to protect jobs by interfering with investment because, 'If a capital is not allowed to get the greatest net revenue that the use of machinery will afford here, it will be carried abroad', leading to 'serious discouragement to the demand for labour'.[6]

By the time of the *Communist Manifesto* in 1848, Marx and Engels could write of the system in terms very similar to those used by people today who regard global competition as a radically new departure:

The need for a constantly expanding market chases the bourgeoisie over the whole surface of the globe. It must nestle everywhere, settle everywhere, establish connections everywhere.

The bourgeoisie has through its exploitation of the world market given a cosmopolitan character to production and consumption in every country. All

old established national industries have been destroyed or daily are being
destroyed. They are dislodged by new industries…that no longer work up
indigenous raw materials, but raw materials drawn from the remotest zones,
industries whose products are consumed not at home, but in every quarter in
the globe… In place of the old local and national seclusion we have inter-
course in every direction, universal interdependence of nations.

The growth of the global operations of capitalism in the second half
of the 19th century were easily as great as those witnessed in the last
three decades. World trade grew by 900 percent by the outbreak of the
First World War—with an average growth rate of about 3.4 percent a
year between 1870 and 1913. Alongside this there was an enormous
growth of international finance, since the financial system was based on
the unrestricted flow of gold from country to country. By the 1880s and
1890s about half of the investment from Britain—still the most powerful
capitalist country—flowed overseas.[7]

The growth rate in international trade in recent years has only been at
about the same pace as a century ago, while governments intervene
much more to influence the flow of goods and capital than they did then.
Exports may have doubled between 1960 and 1990 until they are around
20 percent of world output. But that still means that 80 percent of output
is for markets within the countries where it is produced.

International trade did grow much faster in the 1950s and 1960s than
in the second half of the 19th century—by about 9.9 percent a year until
1973—but this has not been true more recently. And the share of imports
and exports in total output for the three major parts of the advanced
world—the US, Japan and the European Union—has remained more or
less constant for last 15 years.[8] In fact the exception in terms of the
history of capitalism has not been the expansion of international trade,
but rather the fact that it stagnated and even fell for more than 30 years
after 1914. That is: if international trade in 1913 equalled 100; then in
1920-1925 it fell to 82; by 1931-35 it had only risen to 93; and only in
1948 did it rise to 103, just above the 1913 level.

The fall in foreign trade in these years was accompanied by two
breakdowns in the old international monetary system based on gold—
with the outbreak of war in 1914 and then again during the great slump
of the early 1930s. A new international monetary system based upon the
dollar as well as gold, and relying on governments to try and fix their
exchange rates, the 'Bretton Woods' system, came into being at the end
of the Second World War. Since it too broke down in the early 1970s,
currencies have been free to 'float' in value in relation to each other, but
governments (as central banks) have exerted enormous influence by
intervening to buy or sell currencies. The result is that currency levels
are very much dependent upon negotiations between governments (or

central banks), rather than pure market forces. As Mann notes:

> *Domestic saving and investment still correlate about 75 percent among OECD countries, indicating that foreign capital is not all that internationally mobile... And the differences in real interest rates between countries are about the same as they were a century ago. Indeed, it is doubtful whether, in many respects, capital is more transnational than it was before 1914, except in the special case of the European Union.*[9]

More significant than the growth in trade has been the growth in foreign direct investment, which grew four times as fast as trade in the mid-1980s and has been growing twice as fast as trade since.[10] Much of the apparent credibility of the 'globalisation' orthodoxy arises from this phenomenon. It enables the orthodoxy to paint a picture of capital flowing evenly across the face of the earth, ceaselessly shifting from one spot to another in search of lower labour wages and higher profits, with a tendency towards the sprinkling of production facilities uniformly across all five continents.

In fact, however, the real picture of the location of capital is very different to this. Almost all the major multinationals tend to invest more in one country than any other. Of the *Fortune* 100 largest firms, 40 do half or more of their sales in foreign markets, but only 18 maintain the majority of their assets abroad and only 19 at least half their workforce.[11] What is more, the minority of multinationals which have internationalised in this way are usually those based in the smaller European countries—Switzerland, Holland, Sweden—and the 'internationalisation' usually takes the form of investing in industrial regions very close to their own (Dutch capital looking to Britain and Germany, Swiss capital to neighbouring areas of Germany and France, and so on). What is involved is often a 'regionalisation' rather than an internationalisation of capital.

The largest multinationals do not invest evenly across the globe. Most trade and investment is between advanced countries. So in the early 1990s half of cumulative UK foreign direct investment was in the US, 27 percent in Western Europe. For total world overseas investment, three quarters was concentrated in North America, Western Europe or Japan. The ten most important developing countries accounted for a mere 16.5 percent (so much for the story that firms are moving all their money to Singapore or Taiwan), while the rest of the world receives only 8.5 percent. In other words, far from there being a homogenous 'global' arena for investment, nearly two thirds of the world is virtually written off the map as far as direct investment is concerned. As Stopford and Strange have pointed out:

As firms harness the power of new technology to create systems of activity linked directly across borders, so they increasingly concentrate on those territories offering the greatest potential for recovering their investment. Moreover, in a growing number of key sectors, the basis of competition is shifting to emphasising product quality, not just costs. Attractive sites for new investment are increasingly those supplying skilled workers and efficient infrastructures...[12]

What is more, the bulk of investment from firms in one country is concentrated in that and adjacent countries, as the following table for the major multinationals in 1992-1993 shows:

PERCENTAGE OF BUSINESS FOR MULTINATIONALS IN HOME COUNTRY[13]

	manf'g sales	service sales	manf'g assets	service assets
US	64	75	70	74
Japan	75	77	97	92
Germany	48	65	n/a	n/a
France	45	69	55	50
UK	36	61	39	61

The assets of US multinational corporations are mainly concentrated at home, and of Japanese ones overwhelmingly so. In the case of the European powers, the picture is not so very different if the main locations of 'overseas' assets is taken into account—it is overwhelmingly within the other European states. So 31 percent of French manufacturing and 35 percent of French service assets are in other European countries—giving cumulative figures of 86 and 85 percent of assets which are in what might be called France's 'home' region. Figures are not available for the distribution of the assets of German and Italian companies, but the surveys of their behaviour suggest they tend to follow the same 'regional' approach as the French.[14]

For Europe, this picture is confirmed by a 1990 inquiry 'among top managers of 200 large European firms'. It showed they 'planned in the next five years to perform 93 percent of their entire production within Europe, to buy 80 percent of their inputs from European sources and to sell 83 percent of the output to European clients'.[15] As Hirst and Thompson explain:

The extreme concentration of assets in the home country for Japan and the US is apparent... The multinational corporations still rely upon their 'home base' as the centre of all their economic activities, despite all the speculation about globalisation.[16]

The picture is slightly less clear cut in the case of the European multinationals, because many have begun investing in neighbouring European
countries, but if the European Union is treated as a 'home region',
degrees of concentration comparable to those in the US and Japan are
found. British multinationals are an exception, in that over 20 percent of
their assets are in the US, a similar figure to that for continental Europe.
Both figures are, however, much higher than for assets located in the
whole of the rest of the world combined (including the much hyped
Asian 'tigers').

This picture suggests we might be faced not with global integration
but with regional integration within each of the North American,
Japanese and European parts of the advanced industrial world. If that
were so, the in-word 'globalisation' would have to be replaced by the
word 'regionalisation'.[17]

The multinationals

Globalisation 'common sense' stresses the relentless rise of multinationals which it depicts as roaming the world, seeking the cheapest
place for investment in each stage in production processes.

It is a claim which rings true to many people because it starts from
real developments in a number of important industries. And it is not a
claim that can be refuted simply by pointing to the figures for trade and
investment given above—a mistake made by Hirst and Thompson. The
fact that *levels* of foreign trade and foreign investment were higher in
1914 than today does not in itself prove that nothing has changed with
regard to the *organisation* of production. The same billion pounds of
total investment might represent investment in 100 factories competing
with each other, or it might represent investment in a group of factories
each carrying through different parts of a single productive process.

In fact there have been certain changes in production over the last
century which the raw figures for investment do not show. Until the
1880s most industries consisted of a multiplicity of small producing
units. This began to change at the end of the century with the concentration of production within each major country into trusts and combines
which set out to conquer world markets from rivals abroad. But there
was little international integration of manufacturing production, and the
early multinationals tended either to be based on extracting raw materials
from the Third World for manufacture in the West (Unilever or the oil
companies, for example), or on the ownership of foreign subsidiaries
which were involved in completely local production (Ford, for example).

This remained the picture right through until the late 1960s, with a
handful of nationally based (even if sometimes foreign owned) firms,

often closely tied to the state, dominating each major industrial sector inside each country. But then new patterns of production began to emerge. There was a restructuring of industry in ways that could cut across national boundaries and which tended to be associated with the rise of a new wave of European multinationals. The restructuring of industries after the recessions of the mid-1970s and early 1980s was to a large extent restructuring on an international rather than a merely national scale.

But recognising these as major developments, inaugurating a new phase in the history of capitalism, just as the national concentration of capital did at the beginning of the century, is not the same thing as accepting the globalisation orthodoxy. Ruigrok and van Tulder, although writing in a style that is academic in the extreme, have merit over Hirst and Thompson because they see that major changes have been taking place, but insist that they do not lead to the conclusions of the globalisation orthodoxy.

They point out that the rationalisation of production to cope with increased international competition does not mean that all, or even most, multinationals have established integrated production processes right across the world—what we might call 'global assembly lines'.[18] Different multinationals respond in very different ways to the pressures for restructuring. The setting up of global assembly lines is simply one particular response, and not the most common. And many attempts to achieve it have come unstuck. Ford and General Motors did seem to be moving in this direction in the late 1970s when they first talked about the 'world car'. But the concept did not come to fruition, and both corporations continued with production lines in Europe turning out very different cars, using very different components, to the production lines in North America.

Gordon, writing eight years ago, pointed out that figures for the US multinationals do not back up claims that, in general, they relied increasingly on components manufactured by their plants elsewhere in the world:

In 1966, intra-firm trade comprising imports from majority-owned foreign affiliates of US transnational corporations to their US parent equalled 16.8 percent of total US imports. By 1982, the ratio had barely increased, rising to only 17.1 percent.

In 1966, more dramatically, the proportion of total US manufacturing imports accounted for by the involvement of transnational corporations in one form or another was 75 percent. By 1977 that percentage had declined to 58. By 1983 it had further declined to 46.3 percent.

Similarly, among US imports governed by tariff provisions controlling parts assembly abroad, the proportion of total import value represented by value-added abroad equalled 51.7 percent in 1966 and 50.9 percent in 1979, suggesting no increase in the proportion of value-added derived from overseas sites.[19]

He points out, 'Even in the Third World, US multinationals' manufacturing investment is still aimed primarily at production for sale internally, not for export...'[20] Electronics was one industry which seemed, more than any other, to exemplify the global assembly line approach in the 1970s and early 1980s, with chips and other components produced in some Third World countries, assembly taking place in others and final sale in advanced countries—but at least one study suggests there was a reversal of this trend in the mid-1980s:

As chip integration becomes greater, the relative amount of assembly work to be done becomes smaller... These changes reduce the significance of labour costs and hence the attractiveness of Third World locations relative to the economies of co-locating sub-automated assemblies and wafer fabrication in developed countries. Although Third World plants do not seem to be being abandoned, it does appear that advanced country locations are more favoured for new assembly plants... Many of the features of the geography of semiconductor production do not fit the popular radical stereotypes of locational strategies of multinationals and the changing international division of labour.[21]

In fact, most multinationals still rely less on the global assembly line approach than they do on the old one of concentrating their investments within a particular advanced industrial country and its neighbours, and then relying on the sheer scale of investment, research and development and production there to provide an advantage over all competitors, whether nationally based or multinationals. It was in this way, for instance, that Boeing came to dominate the world market for civil aircraft, that the Japanese motor companies clocked up their enormous exports (it was not until the 1990s that Toyota and Nissan began serious overseas investment), and the South Korean shipbuilding industry came to carve out a huge chunk of the world market. Gordon pointed out, 'Since the mid-1960s, the greatest Newly Industrialising Country [NIC] gains have come in heavily capital-intensive industries such as steel, shipbuilding, chemicals and most recently automobiles. The key to these great advances have been massive state investment in capital and dramatic growth in labour productivity'.[22]

Of increasing importance is a third approach. It breaks with the predominantly national basis of production without, however, turning to the 'global assembly line' stereotype. It involves a previously nationally based company seeking to overcome foreign opposition to its success in exporting by establishing locally based plants. These may start off as 'screwdriver plants', devoted simply to assembling components imported from the multinational's home country. But there is then a tendency for them to turn to local firms to provide these components. The firms effectively become satellites of the multinational within the local country, and they fight for its interests against other local or regional competitors. The pattern in this case is not, according to Ruigrok and van Tulder, 'globalisation' as it is normally understood, but glocalisation.

Such a strategy has the great advantage for the firm concerned that its impact on the local market can be substantially greater than the investment it makes, since it in effect mobilises the capital of its local suppliers for its own competitive goals. Its own capital outlays can be much lower than under the 'global assembly line' approach. It also enables the firm to cut down enormously on the cost of supplying its local factories with parts—which is why, under the name 'outsourcing', it is being adopted by Ford and General Motors in both the US and Europe.[23] As the managing director of Samsung's Scottish subsidiary explains:

> *Samsung's European investments start life with an average of 30 percent equity funding from the Korean parent. The rest is locally funded... Samsung has ambitious targets for making its European operations self-sufficient.*
>
> *It takes 40 to 50 days to move products from Korea. The response of the supply chain is critical to our success. The supply chain is also the biggest single element of our cost.*[24]

This partly explains the fact that wages are not the main feature determining where Samsung invests. Its average hourly wage costs vary from about $3 in Malaysia, $10 in Korea and Scotland and $13 in Barcelona to $27 in Berlin.[25] Such a 'Toyotaist' or 'glocalisation' approach by a multinational leads to quite different behaviour to that assumed by the globalisation consensus with its belief in the onward march of global assembly lines.

First, a multinational adopting such an approach is likely be less keen to move any individual investment, since it serves to tie the additional capital of local suppliers to it, than will be a firm for whom any particular investment is just one small fragment of a worldwide production chain. Secondly, while a multinational adopting a 'global assembly line' approach will oppose attempts at protectionism by individual governments or groups of governments, since these can upset its global calculations, 'Toyotaist' multinationals can, as 'local' producers, be indifferent to the protectionist measures of the state in which they have subsidiaries—and even, on occasions, welcome such measures as a way of warding off competition from multinationals based elsewhere. So, for example, Japanese and Korean companies invest in Britain out of fear of the European Union introducing protectionist measures which restrict their exports. But once established here, they can come to feel they will positively gain from such measures, since these will not hit them as 'local producers' but will hit other foreign competitors.

The globalisation orthodoxy fails to differentiate between these quite different ways in which multinationals can react to increased competition because it assumes that the advance of innovation on a world scale always requires the integration of production on a world scale. But this is by no means always true.

Firms in particular countries cannot afford to be cut off from the advances to be obtained from the level of research and development which is available only to a handful of big spenders worldwide. One of the reasons for the eventual failure of the attempts to develop nationally self-contained industries in the old Eastern bloc and in many developing countries was that without access to many new technologies developed in the US and Japan (especially in spheres like microelectronics and computing), their costs of production rose far above the world average. But global assembly lines are not a necessary precondition for the utilisation of all new technologies. Often all that is needed is that a nationally or regionally based industry is linked to a global centre of innovation, while continuing to concentrate production locally. A multinational may have to spend such enormous sums on research and development that it can only recoup them if it produces in as many parts of the world as possible. But that does not mean that it has to establish an integrated worldwide production process. It can cover its outlays just as well if it introduces its new technologies simultaneously into operations that take place in other respects independently of each other in different parts of the world.[26]

There are even cases where firms which used to operate on the 'global assembly line' pattern have shifted to this other approach. A case in point is in oil. For decades this was dominated by the infamous Seven Sisters, multinationals which set out directly to own every stage in the production process, from pumping oil out of the ground to pumping petrol into cars. In the last quarter century they have been forced to change their approach in some ways, under the impact of demands for the takeover of oilfields and establishment of refineries by governments in the oil producing countries and by the rise of state sponsored companies like Elf in France and AGIP in Italy. But this does not mean the old Seven Sisters have suffered. They have been able to use their ability to mobilise resources and technology globally to ensure that even when they do not directly own oilfields or refineries they exercise control over their operations and get a nice slice of the profits.

Globalisation theorists fail to recognise such developments. Yet they often try to bolster their own case by references to investments like those of Japanese motor companies in Britain which are precisely along these lines. And they often refer to the 'flexible production' characteristic, for instance, of part of the Italian knitwear industry, and 'just in time' production methods as typical of globalisation, although, as Mann has quite correctly noted, both imply localised or regional, rather than global, production.[27]

Multinationals and the movement of capital

A central tenet of the 'globalisation' common sense is that multinationals can move their capital whenever they want, so thwarting attempts of governments to control them or of workers to improve wages and conditions. What is involved in this claim is a central confusion between different sorts of capital. It is very easy for firms which trade internationally to move money internationally. But moving money is not same thing as moving productive capital.

Productive capital is made up of factories and machinery, mines, docks, offices and so on. These take years to build up and cannot be simply picked up and carted away. Sometimes a firm can move machinery and equipment. But this is usually an arduous process and, before it can be operated elsewhere, the firm has to recruit or train a sufficiently skilled workforce. In the interim, not only does the investment in the old buildings have to be written off, there is no return on the investment in the machinery either.

What is more, few productive processes are ever completely self-contained. They depend on inputs from outside and links to distribution networks. So, if a firm sets up a car plant, it has to ensure there are secure sources of nuts and bolts, steel of the right quality, a labour force with the right level of training, reliable electricity and water supplies, a trustworthy financial system, friendly bankers, and a road and rail network capable of shifting its finished products. It has to persuade other people—other firms or governments—to provide these things, and the process of assembling them can take months or even years of bargaining, involving trial and error as well as forward planning. Multinationals do not just throw these assets away and hope to find them thousands of miles away because labour is slightly cheaper or governments are slightly more co-operative. Such moves take time and effort and involve writing off existing 'sunk costs'. Productive capital simply cannot be footloose.

In practice most capitalist enterprises operate not simply on market calculations, but also on the long term relations they establish with other enterprises that sell to them and buy from them. Otherwise they would live in continual fear that any change in market conditions would cause their suppliers to sell elsewhere and those who transport and retail their goods suddenly to lose interest in them. They seek to 'lock in' these other firms by a combination of financial incentives, business favours and personal contact.

Ruigock and van Tulder emphasise this point by insisting that production does not take place in individual firms, but in 'industrial complexes', which have grown up over years and which are not easily dismantled piecemeal: 'Neither individual firms nor states but industrial complexes constitute the centre of gravity of the international restructuring race'.[28]

Of course, firms do shift the location of their plants, and future investments do not always occur in the same places as past investments. Restructuring does often involve shutting old plants and opening new ones. But decisions to do such things are never taken lightly and always incur some costs. For this reason, when restructuring firms usually prefer the road of 'gradualism'—of moving piecemeal from old plant to new, keeping intact old supply and distribution networks, minimising the dislocation to the 'complex' around them.

Job losses and the movement of capital

The claim that the movement of capital to less developed countries in search of lower labour costs has been the *main* cause of rising unemployment in the advanced countries is hardly borne out by the facts. Of course there have been some such job losses. But the publicity given to particular cases—like that of British Airways moving some of its computing to India—should not lead anyone to believe this is the main explanation for high unemployment levels. After all, even in the British Airways, the total number of jobs lost since privatisation has been 17,000; the number of computer operators taken on by British Airways in India is 130.[29] Something else is behind the loss of the other 16,870 jobs.

The pattern of investment by the multinationals certainly does not provide a picture of massive investment in cheap labour countries at the expense of jobs in the advanced countries. Quite the opposite, as noted above—the bulk of direct foreign investment by multinationals is in the advanced industrial countries. This is for the simple reason that the multinationals have found these the most profitable countries to invest in:

> In the mid-1970s the average rate of return for US corporations on their direct foreign investments in manufacturing in developing countries was somewhat higher than the corresponding rate of return in developed coun-

tries; by 1985, the manufacturing rate of return on US foreign direct invest-
ment in the less developed countries had declined to only two thirds of its
level in developed countries.[30]

What is more, the developing countries which have witnessed the
biggest surges of investment have not, in general, been those with the
lowest wages. So while most of the poorest continent, Africa, stagnates
and experiences an outflow of capital, growth has continued at a relatively rapid rate in countries like South Korea which have relatively high
wages (only a little lower on average than those in Britain). There has
been a substantial movement of relatively low skill industries, like cheap
textiles and footwear, clothing and basic household goods (the sort of
things sold in 'eveything for £1' shops), to the low wage economies of
India and especially China. But production of higher grade textiles and
footwear, white goods (fridges, cookers etc), motors, aircraft, machine
tools, and so on remains concentrated within the advanced countries,
while there has even been a certain tendency of electronics to move back
to the advanced countries.

Overall imports to advanced OECD countries from non-OECD countries grew from about 1 percent to about 2 percent of Gross Domestic
Product between 1982 and 1992. But these figures cannot explain unemployment levels ranging from 6 percent to 20 percent right across the
advanced OECD countries. At most a few hundred thousand of the tens of
millions of jobs destroyed over the last two decades can be ascribed directly
to manufactured imports replacing domestically produced products.

There is other evidence which proves the same point. Unemployment
in the last two decades has not just hit jobs in industries subject to competition from imports. The demand for unskilled labour, in particular, has
fallen in almost all industries. Among those most severely hit are those
where import penetration is necessarily small or non-existent—
construction, newspaper printing, dock work, the civil service, post and
telecoms, refuse disposal, and a host of others. Loss of jobs in these
industries can only be due to firms seeking to raise profits by cost cutting
and new technology on the one hand and recurrent recessions on the
other.

This was borne out by two studies of job loss in the US in the late
1970s and early 1980s. One looked at changes in manufacturing employment between 1972 and 1980. It found that the stagnation of the
economy was responsible for a decline of 1.5 percent in manufacturing
employment, while change in foreign trade caused a 2.1 percent growth
of manufacturing jobs. The other study claimed that 20 percent of job
loss between 1973 and 1980 was directly due to imports, but 64 percent
to lack of demand in the US economy.[31]

The economist Adrian Wood of Sussex University claims that Third

World exports are responsible for a substantial portion of unemployment in the advanced countries, claiming they have led to 'a fall of 20 percent in demand for unskilled labour across the developed world'.[32] But even he does not try to put the blame directly on imports replacing jobs. Instead he claims they reduce jobs indirectly, prompting firms to move to new labour saving technology so as to remain profitable and competitive. In other words, it is rationalisation that is mainly destroying jobs, not imports from, or the movement of capital to, low wage economies.

Multinationals and states

The globalisation argument assumes that capital is increasingly dispensing with the services of a national state. Hirst and Thompson, and Ruigrok and van Tulder challenge this contention by providing a mass of evidence about the continuing dependence on each multinational on a 'national base' and on the operations of the state within that national base:

(i) First, as we have seen, the majority of multinationals continue to concentrate most of their production within one state, or at least within one state and its close neighbours.

(ii) Even the investment which does flow towards 'cheap labour' locations outside the advanced countries is not completely independent of the operations of the home state. Hirst and Thompson point out that multinationals from each of the major states tend to concentrate their Third World and NIC investment and sales in particular regions of the world where that state exercises influence. So German capital flows to Eastern Europe; French to Central, Western and Northern Africa; the US to certain countries in Latin American; Japan to the Pacific, and so on. 'The direction of foreign direct investment relationships is between one or other of the...powers and its clustered "client" states, rather than between these client states themselves.' Ruigrok and van Tulder note that at least ten 'leading core firms' have modelled their internationalisation strategy 'partly on the geo-political patterns of colonial rule (Royal Dutch/Shell, BP, Unilever, Elf-Aquitaine, Alcatel-Alsthom, Total, ICI, BAe, Petrofina, BTR)'.

(iii) Even where production takes place internationally, research and development are concentrated in the home base. So even the most internationalised firms, those from Holland, Sweden and Switzerland, 'still conduct most of their R & D at home'—two thirds for Swiss firms, 75 percent for 20 leading Swedish multinationals'. Patel and Pavitt found in studies of globalisation of technology, based on looking at patent applications, that 'in most cases the technological activities of large firms are concentrated in their home country'.[33]

(iv) The state continues to played a key role in establishing and maintaining many key firms:

> At least 20 companies in the 1993 **Fortune** 100 would not have survived at all
> as independent companies if they had not been saved by their respective governments in the last decade and a half. Among the most important cases have
> been the British, French and Italian steel firms in the early 1980s, Chrysler in
> the early 1980s, and McDonnel Douglas, VW's SEAT subsidiary.
>
> As recently as 1993 the Swedish government came to the support of the
> **Skandinaviska Enskilda Banken** (the Wallenberg consortium's family bank)
> and the **Handelsbanken**, Sweden's two major banks with large holdings in
> Swedish production companies such as Volvo, Electrolux, Ericsson, Asea,
> **Stora**, and SKF. The Wallenberg consortium alone accounts for 40 percent of
> the Stockholm stock exchange.[34]

Similarly, it was the South Korean state which saved Daewoo from going bust in 1987. On top of this, all the key telecoms firms depend for major contracts on governments—and bargaining between governments and international consortia—as of course do defence industry firms. 'All formerly or currently leading US computers, semiconductors and electronic makers in 1993 *Fortune* 100 have benefitted enormously from preferential defence contracts'.[35]

(v) Last, but not least, 23 of the *Fortune* 100 in 1993 were 'directly engaged in the oil industry'[36]—an industry which is notoriously dependent on the military hegemony exercised by the US to ward off threats to its operations in the Middle East.

The restructuring of industry to meet increased international competition by no means spells the end of the dependence of firms on states over which they exercise a special influence. Indeed, the very competitiveness of the global economy can increase the reliance of multinationals on governments, as Stopford and Strange have insisted in a study of the relations between the two:

> Growing interdependence now means that the rivalry between states and the
> rivalry between firms for a secure place in the world economy has become
> much fiercer, much more intense. As a result, firms have become more
> involved with governments and governments have come to realise their
> increased dependence on the scarce resources controlled by firms.[37]

So the 'Toyotaist' firms, which build parallel production units in different parts of the world can only hegemonise local firms (rather than be subject to pressures from them) if domination in key areas like research and development gives them the upper hand when it comes to bargaining. But this means keeping these activities where they can be tightly controlled, in their 'home base' country, with a state that can be relied on to defend their interests in international negotiations over 'intellectual copyright'.

But it is not only 'home' governments which are important to multinationals. Whenever they have made a substantial investment in any country, the policies of its government become an important factor to them—providing them with subsidies, creating an amenable tax regime for them, providing infrastructure links, educating a workforce with necessary skills, and so on. They can lose out substantially if they cannot bend the government to their will, and so they tend to become dependent on it just as it becomes dependent on them. This provides governments with a degree of leverage over multinationals, even if, for political reasons, they often claim otherwise. Again, as Stopford and Strange note:

> Only a few firms can operate in a "borderless" world. Governments, both host and home, continue to play a crucial and, perhaps paradoxically, an increasing role.[38]

A world of non-national capitals?

'The nationalities of companies are becoming increasingly irrelevant', claimed Britain's chancellor Kenneth Clark when he was industry minister back in 1988.[39] It is a claim which has been repeated by many other proponents of the globalisation thesis. Yet the empirical evidence to back it up is thin indeed. The capitalists of any country today do fly from one part of the world to another negotiating deals, do run front companies in a score of financial capitals and offshore islands, shifting funds from one to another as they commute from one holiday home to another. There is emerging what Stopford and Strange call 'a privileged transnational business civilisation',[40] the embryo of a single, world, ruling class.

But the control of any major multinational firm remains firmly anchored in the hands of capitalists from a particular country, as Ruigrok and van Tulder prove by a mass of empirical research. Of 30 US 'core' firms, only five had a foreigner on their executive board in 1991, and only 2 percent of board members of big American companies were foreigners. Only two out of 20 big Japanese companies had a foreigner of their board. Of 15 'core' German firms, only four had a foreigner on their management board.[41]

Even share ownership is much more nationally concentrated than is implied by all the talk about 'global markets'. Ruigrok and van Tulder note that few 'core firms have over 10 percent of their shares owned abroad', with most Japanese and Korean firms not even bothering to have their shares listed on foreign stock markets, while most overseas holdings of German shares are in German speaking Switzerland and Austria[42]. Dutch, Swedish and Swiss multinationals have been forced to internationalise their productive activities because of the smallness of their national base economy, but 'Many of them remain remarkably nationalistic in many respects… They do not distinguish themselves by listing on foreign stock exchanges…' and they 'tend to have only a few non-nationals on their top management boards… By 1994, only Phillips had a really internationalised top management board'.[43]

If firms do not encourage international share ownership and control, neither is it easy for individual investors in one country to invest profitably in multinationals based elsewhere. As Peter Martin of the *Financial Times* recently noted in an article *extolling* 'the creation of a homogenous global economy':

> It will always be easier to find out what is happening inside a company based locally than to scrutinise a business with headquarters on the other side of the world… Currency risk is more difficult still. An investor…would…face the potential mismatch between the currency in which his assets were denominated and the currency in which his spending was likely to occur.[44]

Assessing the argument

The core of the evidence marshalled against the 'globalisation' consensus cannot be challenged. The system is international, but it always has been. Firms will seek out the most profitable sites internationally for production, but this does not mean they are 'footloose' and able to abandon existing sites at a moment's notice, nor does it mean that they always go to where labour is cheapest. There is a tendency to restructure production across national boundaries, but this does not prevent multinationals relying on national and regional bases for launching out into the wider world and it by no means always implies the setting up of worldwide production lines. Capitalist states are restricted in their ability to control the working of the system they support, but this does not mean they are irrelevant to it.

Yet the conclusions Mann, Hirst and Thompson draw are wrong in two inter-related respects.

First, they see the limitations of the globalisation common sense as leaving room for a return to national reformism—or even regional and global reformism. Thus Mann suggests that there is a 'Nordic' way of

coping with increased global competition through 'a high skills, high
education, high tech strategy requiring large government expenditures'
which would lead to 'higher national wealth',[45] while stability is possible
internationally through 'trilateral arrangements between US, Japanese
and dual German-European governmental institutions, sometimes
embedded in the wider G7 nations', making it possible for 'the centre-
piece of Enlightenment modernity, world peace' at last to come 'to
fruition, at least in one part of the world'.[46]

Hirst and Thompson are even more explicit about their continuing
belief in the efficacy of piecemeal reform. They believe governments
can bring order to the economy through a slight adjustment to the traditional techniques. All that is required, they argue, is for these
governments to extend their present 'economic summits' into systematic
co-operation. If only the 'G3' (the US, Japan and 'Europe') lay down
rules for the money markets and direct investment, the resulting 'governance' will begin to bring the system to order. Then other national
governments, and within them provincial and urban authorities, will be
able to 'orchestrate consensus' in which 'the different factors of production relate to each other in other than just market terms, ie labour and
management and capital providers and firms'.

All this is a pipe dream—and a pipe dream which leads to reactionary
conclusions. The economic summits show no signs of being able to regulate the world economy, still less to turn it in a rational direction. They
are, in fact, horse trading sessions in which the rival governments push
the interests of the rival firms connected to them. They take concerted
action when their interests happen to coincide (for instance, when it
comes to opening up some other country to their joint exploitation), or
when the most powerful of them (the US) succeeds in browbeating the
others into accepting its hegemony (dressed up as 'a new world order').
More often than not, however, it is not concerted action that results, but
a failure to agree—'the new world disorder'.

To call for greater 'governance' by these bodies is to push for them to
have more power to subjugate the rest of the world to the interests of the
most powerful capitalists, and within that, to push for an even greater
dominance of US capitalism. The talk of 'Europe' as an 'economic'
power is also in the realm of fantasy. Europe is not one entity, but a
squabbling coalition of rival states, whose capitalists confront one
another as well as those of the US and Japan. At times this confrontation
means alliances to carve up markets, but at other times acrimonious disputes as these alliances break apart and new, rival ones are formed.

There are, of course, powerful interests pressing for a more integrated
European capitalism, and with it the beginnings of a cohesive European
state. But these interests are not looking to a peaceful, harmonious and

humane world presided over by the sort of 'governance' that would make people's lives better. Rather they are intent on establishing a Europe in which the untrammelled dominance of capital is protected by the Maastricht criteria and a central bank immune to any sort of elected control.

The second fault in their account concerns their interpretation of the history of the system in the 20th century. As we have seen, Hirst and Thompson's stress on quantitative growth figures for international trade and investment ignores important changes that occurred from one period to another in the qualitative organisation of production. They also make no real attempt to account for what happened in the period from the First World War through to the beginning of the 1950s in which international trade and investment fell—a period which saw a tendency right across the world for growing integration between capital and the state, or, as Bukharin and Lenin described it, for 'state capitalism'.

Hirst and Thompson share the same view as most globalisation theorists in their assessment of this period. They see state intervention as government action, under the pressure of public opinion, to ward off slump, using 'Keynesian' methods of economic management. But while the globalisation theorists believe there has been a radical change which has taken such power away from states, Hirst and Thompson believe that states still have that power if only they can bring themselves to use it.

Underlying both positions is a misunderstanding about what actually happened during the high tide of state capitalism. Governments right across the world talked of 'economic planning', did nationalise certain industries, and did wrest, to a greater or less extent, decisions over investment from individual capitalists.[47] And in the latter part of this period, from the 1940s to the early 1970s, there was both an unprecedented boom and an unprecedented rise in the living standards of workers—what has been called by some writers 'the golden age of capitalism'.

But the boom and rising living standards were not a result either of Keynesianism or of government intervention under the pressure of public opinion. Governments found themselves quite incapable of boosting the economy when their main motivation for doing so was to deal with the mass unemployment and poverty created by economic slump. Mann quite rightly notes that, long before anyone talked of 'globalisation':

> *It is doubtful whether reformist politicians had much used their 'potential' power to manipulate currency and interest rates to freely spend and redistribute. They did so mostly in the peculiar circumstances of the aftermath of two world wars... At most other times they seem to have been really quite disciplined by capitalist orthodoxies and by the spectre of capital flight and*

currency fluctuations... I think...of the complete collapse of leftist political economy before international capitalist pressures in countries like Britain, Germany or Spain from 1929 onwards. I remain unconvinced that the international capitalist pressures on the nation state are uniquely threatening in the contemporary period. The pressures have always been there.[48]

And it was not, as Mann suggests, a mere lack of will power on the part of reformist governments that led to such failures. They were, in fact, trapped by the logic of reformism itself, which involved trying to make the system work—and that meant subordinating their policies to the demands of capitalist accumulation. So it was that programmes for intervention governments were only effective in the years between the 1930s and the 1970s when they facilitated accumulation or the drive to military competition. They were ineffective when their prime motivation was to provide reforms in the interests of the mass of the population.

This explains why the rise of state intervention—the trend towards greater or lesser degrees of state capitalism—was inseparable from preparation for war, preparations which in the 1930s were accompanied by attacks rather than improvements in the living standards and working conditions of the mass of people. It was only when war preparations had, as an unintended consequence, turned slump to boom, that living standards and working conditions began to improve in countries like Britain and the US.

The dominant economic orthodoxy of the period turned reality on its head, ascribing the boom to its own 'Keynesian' views. But examination of the empirical record for these years shows that government intervention in the advanced countries from the 1940s right through to 1973 was designed to slow down boom rather than to overcome recession.[49]

In less economically advanced parts of the world there was greater leeway for intervention, since local capitalist classes were relatively weak. Groups not necessarily from the established capitalist class could get control of the state and push through a programme of statifying local capital in order to industrialise, transforming themselves into a state capitalist class. This happened in Eastern Europe after 1945, in China, Vietnam and Cuba, and also in countries like Argentina, Egypt, Syria, Iraq and Algeria.

Typically, regimes used the direct power of the state to limit the number of direct ties with foreign capitalists, and to prolong booms by moving physical outputs from 'non-priority' to 'priority' sections of the economy every time tendencies towards slump began to appear. These regimes talked of planning and usually described themselves as some sort of socialism ('Communism', 'Arab socialism', 'African socialism', 'Islamic socialism', even 'royal socialism'). But since the 'non-priority' sectors were invariably those which concerned workers' and peasants' living standards, this was certainly not a case of the state intervening to promote the needs of the mass of the population. It was, in fact, one way by which the state subordinated the internal economy to the military or market pressures on it from the rest of the world capitalist system. The 'autonomy' of the state consisted in being able to pick and choose exactly how it imposed the dynamic of the world system on the local population, not in being able to turn its back on that dynamic.

There were further important changes in the world system from the mid-1970s onwards. But these changes did not remove from the state some magical power to act as if the rest of the world system did not exist. Rather they shifted the most effective ways for states to foster the accumulation of nationally based capitalism (whether 'state' or 'private') in the face of the pressures from the system as whole,

Reducing the internal economy's direct links with foreign capital had enabled many states to oversee a high tempo of capital accumulation for a generation or more. But now this became an increasingly costly option because it restricted the possibilities of gaining access to the new technologies which were in the hands of the world's biggest foreign firms. Whereas it seemed from the early 1930s to the early 1960s that, the further economies had gone in the direction of state capitalism, the greater were their rates of growth, by the 1980s it seemed the other way round. Regimes were under enormous pressure to allow internal capital to link up directly with capitals elsewhere in the world system—borrowing from foreign banks, forming alliances with foreign multinationals in return for access to new technologies, importing a growing range of capital equipment and components, paying for these things with ever greater emphasis on sales in foreign markets.

This happened just as the world economy as a whole entered into a new period of crises from 1974 onwards. Governments which had paid lip service to Keynesian techniques without needing to use them during the long boom now had to confront recession and found that these techniques did not work.

States found they could not protect national capitalist accumulation from world crisis just at the time when world crisis itself was back with a vengeance. This was devastating for the most thoroughgoing state capitalisms, those usually labelled as 'socialist' in the Eastern bloc and parts of the Third World.[50] It was just as devastating for reformists who believed that social democratic politics based on Keynesian prescriptions were the way forward in the advanced Western states. In Britain the Labour government had abandoned such prescriptions by summer 1976. In France Mitterrand followed six years later. The popularity of 'globalisation' notions was born as experience refuted the belief that reform of the system carried through from above could stop crises afflicting a national economy. But, instead of recognising that this belief had always been mistaken, 'globalisation' theories see it as a new feature.

In fact, what we confront today is not some immense new power in the hands of international capital, but a power which goes back at least as far as Ricardo. It is the power to tell those who try to reform any part of the world system that they must abide by the laws created by its dynamic of competitive accumulation. The only successes reformism can claim have been in periods like the late 1940s, the 1950s and the early 1960s when even countries with avowedly pro-capitalist parties in government, like West Germany, Italy or the US, provided reforms that benefitted workers. By contrast, whenever the system has gone through long periods of crisis, reformist governments have been impotent, and their ministers have tried to excuse themselves by pointing to 'international' forces beyond their control. Thus Ramsay MacDonald told Labour's conference in 1930 there was little his government could do:

> So my friends, we are not on trial. It is the system under which we live. It has broken down, not only in this little island; it has broken down in Europe, in Asia, in America; it has broken down everywhere as it was bound to break down.[51]

The argument of the 'Austro-Marxist' and former German finance minister Rudolf Hilferding was virtually identical: 'The basic problem is that we are unable to tell the people in a concrete manner how we will eliminate the crisis, what immediately successful means we would employ...'[52] 'Too much', he contended, 'was out of the hands of German social democracy, out of the hands of anybody: the economic crisis was international'.[53]

MacDonald and Hilferding did not use the 'g' word, but their basic excuse for abandoning promises to improve the conditions of the mass of workers was essentially the same as that used by reformist politicians today—that the power of the international system is too great for government action to make any difference.

There is a simple answer to such arguments, whether in their 1930s form or in their 1990s form. Reformist governments cannot cope with the crisis because they accept the constraints of the system. They are willing to leave the major means of production in existing hands, and insofar as they attempt to limit the power of capital (exchange controls, regulation of investment, public expenditure programmes) they do so from the top down, through existing state machines—machines built on the assumption of collaboration with capital, not opposition to it, and dominated at the top by those who identify with the interests of capital. In the reformist perspective, there is no place for the direct action of workers from below. Yet it is precisely such action which, if co-ordinated right across the economy, can prevent actions by capital (movements of capital abroad, closure of factories, hoarding of necessities) designed to sabotage attempts to improve the condition of the mass of the people—and can then go further, to put the means of production to work in ways designed to satisfy need, not the drive for profit.

Of course this then leads us back to the problem of revolution in one country. A single country, however large, does not have within it the means to establish the society of plenty which is the precondition for socialism. Such means have been established by capitalism on a world scale, and any country which is cut off indefinitely from the rest of the world, far from being able to supersede capitalism, will *in the long run* succumb to its pressures. But that does not mean in the short run it cannot manoeuvre to maintain itself while pushing through economic changes to the advantage of the great majority of its people (redistribution of wealth from the rich to the masses, redirection of waste production towards people's needs, putting into use means of production which are left idle under capitalism because they are not sufficiently profitable, etc) and using its resources to encourage similar change in other countries.

How successful it is will depend on a variety of contingent factors—how large it is, how much it depends for its immediate survival on resources outside its boundaries, the degree to which the great powers opposed to the changes it has pushed through are divided among themselves, above all, the degree to which it is able to promote revolutionary ferment in other countries.

The important point here, however, is that the changes in capitalism that conventionally go under the name 'globalisation' do not make such an attempt at a revolutionary breakthrough qualitatively more difficult. For instance, the question of dependence on resources outside the state border was a central issue during the revolutionary wave at the end of the First World War. Bolshevik Russia suffered enormously through being cut off from the coal mines of German occupied Ukraine and the oil of British occupied Baku; Germany was suffering from an acute shortage of food at the beginning of 1919; even a revolution in the most advanced European capitalism at the time, Britain, would have faced the problem of the dependence of the national economy on trade. For reformists these were all arguments, then, as now, for accepting the parameters laid down by capitalism; for revolutionaries they were arguments for having a perspective of seizing power and then spreading the revolution.

The global economy and the power of workers

It is not only reformist governments which are powerless, according to the 'globalisation' consensus. Workers too, it is said, have much less ability to stand up to the dictates of capital than in the past. This is an argument against any attempt by a workers' government to break with the system. But it is also an argument about the futility of workers fighting even for the most minimal of reforms within the existing system—whether welfare reforms or improvements in wages or working conditions from the employer. Any attempt by workers seriously to impose their demands on capital will simply lead to it ignoring them and, if necessary, decamping elsewhere in the system.

But, as we saw earlier, industrial capital is not footloose. It can, of course, move in the long run, but only if it is prepared to pay a high price. What is more, the very international integration on which the globalisation consensus places such a stress *increases* the bargaining power of particular groups of workers. In the genuine global assembly line, a group of workers producing a single component in virtually any country could, in principle, bring a whole world industry to a halt. In fact, as we have seen, the global assembly line is quite rare. But concentration on a 'regional' basis is increasingly common—and so too is the experience of a quite small group of workers bringing a whole multinational to a halt. This happened in 1988 when Ford workers in Britain struck and brought the whole of Ford Europe to halt within three or four days. It happened again more recently when a relatively small group of workers at one component plant halted all of General Motors' North American operations.

Workers have suffered many defeats over the last two decades. But very few of them have been because capital has simply been able to pack up its bags and move elsewhere. Usually they have been because firms have been able to keep production going in existing plants, or, sometimes, in new plants a few miles away. Thus the defeat of print workers by Rupert Murdoch's News International in 1987 was based on opening up new premises a little more than a mile from the old—and could have been avoided if print union leaders had been prepared to stop production at the old plant before Murdoch was ready to move. They would then have hit Murdoch's newspaper operation in Britain and, in doing so, paralysed the money making machine he depended on to pay interest on his enormous global debts. Cowardice, incompetence or lack of solidarity by union leaders, rather than the sheer power of the multinationals, was similarly behind the defeat of the British miners in 1985, the cross channel seafarers in 1988, the dockers in 1989. It also explains many of the defeats inflicted on US workers—the air traffic controllers at Reagan's hands, the defeats at Hormel in Iowa, at Staley in southern

Illinois, and so on. Capital won, not because it was footloose, but because it fought ruthlessly while the union leaderships preached moderation and respectability.

'Globalisation' of production did not play a significant role in enabling the employers to win any of these disputes. But the ideology of 'globalisation' has played a role. It has encouraged the idea that multinationals are too powerful to be hit by 'old fashioned' forms of workers' struggle—and the abandonment of these forms of struggle has handed victory to the multinationals.

The shape of things to come

There is one final conclusion that the globalisation consensus can lead to: that the system, although uncontrollable, is less dangerous than in the past. This is because states, with their heavily armed military forces, are supposed to be of decreasing relevance to capitalism. It may need a state to protect it against revolt from below, to deal with 'rogue' regimes which will not obey the normal rules of the game, to guarantee the sanctity of contracts and to provide certain parts of the infrastructure. But capitalism does not need rival states which disturb the free movement of capital and trade. It should be able to settle for one hegemonic power (presumably the US) which will supervise a world order in which free trade is increasingly the norm and in which military conflict plays a more marginal role.

The refutation of the consensus should lead to a very different view of the way in which the world system is going, one which is characterised by international conflicts and wars as well as by uncontrollable economic crises. Different firms have different interests and will look to the individual states over which they have influence to achieve these.

There are firms which will look to establishing global domination though free trade—either from nationally based production which can put down all competitors or by global assembly lines. This is clearly the perspective of very important sections of US business, and of some British based multinationals prepared to operate in alliance with them. But even in the case of these firms, their 'national' state—and especially the Pentagon with its huge arms contracts—is of key importance in sustaining production. It is their national state, too, that they depend on to enforce their interests against others when it comes to shaping the system as a whole. Hence, for instance, the protracted efforts by the US state to get enforcement of 'intellectual copyright' during the last GATT negotiations, and its insistence that international agencies like the IMF, the World Bank and the World Trade Organisation endorse a 'free trade' approach to economic development.

Other firms can, however, follow different strategies for conquering world markets—strategies which imply a different attitude to the role of states. So most Japanese firms built up their global presence by exporting from within an economy in which the national state and national business practices provided them with a strong degree of protection. Then, at a certain point, faced with threats of tariffs or quotas from other states—threats to which they often reacted by conceding 'voluntary restraints' on exports—they have begun to turn to production through local subsidiaries (the 'Toyotaist' or 'glocalisation' approach). Once this is done, they can quite happily accept, even encourage, protectionism from the local state as a way of warding off competition from rival multinationals based elsewhere.

German and French firms are tending to expand from their national bases into neighbouring parts of Europe, which leads them to look to a regional European policy to be enacted through strengthened European institutions rather than to worldwide free trade.

None of these strategies means we are witnessing a turn towards the division of the world into virtually self-contained national or regional economies, as tended to happen in the 1930s. World trade goes on rising. But it is not *free* trade, based on non-interference by states, so much as 'negotiated trade', in which states continually pressurise each other to concede the demands of the capitals associated with them.

Much of British capitalism stands in a category of its own. Ruigrok and van Tulder point out that it is the only advanced industrial country with 'weak cohesion'.[54] There are an exceptionally high number of foreign investors in the domestic economy and they come in nearly equal numbers from the US and the European Union.[55] At the same time, the British based multinationals carry out a much higher proportion of production abroad than is the case with those from the other large advanced countries—and again this production is not concentrated in one region, but is divided almost equally between Europe and North America, with a smaller amount in East Asia.

These facts perhaps explain the enthusiasm for talk about 'globalisation' in Britain. Writers are generalising to the whole of world capitalism from the experience of one, declining, sector. But, in the process, they are not taking into account the complexity of that experience. For some of the investment is from multinationals which have worldwide production strategies (for instance, IBM), but the fastest growing investments are from multinationals which have Europe wide strategies (not just the European firms, but also the American and Far Eastern motor firms). And, at the same time, there are key British based multinationals (BAe, GEC, Plessey, Rolls Royce) which are dependent on the considerable military spending of the British state for much of their research and development and a significant chunk of their markets.

These divergent perspectives of different sections of multinational capital in Britain lead to quite different interpretations of the international strategy which should be followed by the national state, particularly when it comes to the attitude to Economic and Monetary Union in Europe. For some sections such union is a natural corollary to their increasingly European organisation of production. For others it could turn into a dangerous obstacle to their global ambitions. The argument is not between those who rely on the state to do their bidding and those who do not. It is rather between different strategies for using the state, one which sees it as a base from which to negotiate global deals, and one which puts the stress on European restructuring. And the picture is further complicated by the presence of important sections of medium and small industry which still operate within an overwhelmingly national perspective.

The fashionable talk about 'globalisation' cannot throw light on these divisions because it fails to distinguish the quite different ways in which different firms restructure in the face of international competition. And if it obscures rather than illuminates issues in Britain, the most internationalised of the major economies, it completely misleads in the case of the other economies. Developments in the world system may be changing the relations between states and firms. But they are not leading to a loss of connection of firms to states, and neither are they leading the major capitals that battle for world dominance to lose a certain national hue.

This is not the world portrayed by globalisation theory, based on the 'neo-classical' model of a system made up of evenly distributed atoms of capital which interact freely with each other. Rather it is a world in which a limited number of states and multinationals press against each other, pushing and pulling as each tries to cajole others to do its will, like giant octopuses with intertwined tentacles. And the cajoling is not restricted merely to economic manoeuvres, for this remains a world in which the biggest industrial states insist on retaining their military capacity, despite the end of the Cold War, and the fastest growing of the East Asian NICs are involved in an arms race with each other and with their neighbours.

The system is unstable and dangerous precisely because capitals retain ties to states, with the possibility of a resort to force continuing to play an important role as multinationals battle each other for global dominance. The fact that the force is normally deployed outside the advanced countries themselves does not diminish its horrific effects on local populations or its destabilising impact on the system as a whole. The bombing of Baghdad is as much part of the logic of the system as the Multifibre Trade Agreement or haggling over royalties for using the latest software.

Globalisation theory cannot see this. Nor can those reformists like Hirst and Thompson who are nostalgic for a mythical Keynesian past, however correct the individual points they make against globalisation theory. But it is something revolutionary socialists have to be able to understand. It means that economic crises always express themselves in political convulsions. And it also means that the struggle is not just against material deprivation, but for the very survival of humanity, for socialism against barbarism.

Notes

1 N Harris, *The End of the Third World* (London, 1986), p198.
2 *Tribune*, 21 June 1996.
3 D Gordon, 'The Global Economy', *New Left Review* 168 (March/April 1988); P Hirst and G Thompson, *Globalisation in question* (London, 1996); M Mann, 'As the twentieth century ages', *New Left Review* 214 (1995); W Ruigrok and R van Tulder, *The Logic of International Restructuring* (London, 1995).
4 At the Socialist Workers Party's 'Marxism' event in 1978.
5 As, for example, the great economic historian Ferdinand Braudel describes graphically in *The Wheels of Commerce* (the second volume of his *Civilisation and Capitalism* trilogy) (New York, 1982).
6 D Ricardo, *On the Principles of Political Economy and Taxation* (Cambridge, 1995), p39.
7 Figures for international trade and investment flows are given in P Hirst and G Thomson, op cit, and in W Ruigrok and R van Tulder, op cit, p124.
8 P Hirst and G Thomson, op cit, pp 19-22.
9 M Mann, op cit, pp117-118.
10 Figures on growth of foreign direct investment are given in P Hirst and G Thomson, op cit, p128.
11 W Ruigrok and R van Tulder, op cit, p156.
12 J Stopford and S Strange, *Rival States, Rival Firms* (Cambridge, 1991), p1.
13 Table based on figures in P Hirst and G Thompson, op cit, pp91-94.
14 W Ruigrok and R van Tulder, op cit, p128.
15 Ibid, p159.
16 P Hirst and G Thompson, op cit, p95.
17 In fact, as I have argued previously there are strong counter-tendencies which continually disrupt 'regional' integration. This is especially apparent in the case of Britain, where, on the one hand, investment to the US is just as important for the major firms as investment to the rest of Europe, while on the other hand inward investment from Japan is significant in certain industrial sectors. And even in the cases of France and Germany, the trend to European integration is countered by a continuing trend to the concentration of capital into rival nationally integrated blocs in industries like engineering and aerospace. See my 'The State and Capital Today', in *International Socialism* 51.
18 Ruigrok and van Tulder use the expression 'macrofordism'—but also apply it to integration of production on a continental basis in Europe as well as global integration.
19 G Thomson, op cit, p49.
20 Ibid, p50.
21 A Sayer, 'Industrial location on a world scale', in Scott and Storpfer (eds), *Production, Work, Territory* (Boston, 1986), pp116-120.

22   D Gordon, op cit, p52.
23   See, for instance, the account of Ford's plans for its Halewood plant in Liverpool,
      'Roller Coaster Ride for Mersey Plant', *The Guardian*, 19 September 1996.
24   *Financial Times*, 21 October 1996.
25   Ibid.
26   This was a distinction I for one failed to make in the past: see the relevant passage
      in *Explaining the Crisis* (London, 1984).
27   M Mann, op cit, p117.
28   W Ruigrok and R van Tulder, op cit, p164. The argument is very similar to that I
      myself put in 'The State and Capital Today' in *International Socialism* 51:
      'Any productive capital grows up within the confines of a particular territory,
      alongside other sibling capitals (they are, as Marx describes them, 'warring
      brothers'). They are mutually dependent on each other for resources, finance and
      markets. And they act together to try to shape the social and political conditions in
      that territory to suit their own purposes... 'The national state and different
      nationally based capitals grow up together, like children in a single family. The
      development of one inevitably shapes the development of the others...'
          'The groups of capitals and the state with which they are associated form a
      system, in which each affects the others. The specific character of each capital is
      influenced by its interaction with the other capitals and the state. It reflects not
      only the general drive to expand value, to accumulate, but also the specific
      environment way in which it has grown up. The state and the individual capitals
      are intertwined, with each feeding off the other... The market models of classical
      and neo-classical economics portray capitals as isolated atoms which engage in
      blind competition with other capitals. In the real world, capitalists have always
      tried to boost their competitive positions by establishing alliances with each other
      and with ambitious political figures—alliances cemented by money, but also by
      intermarriage, old boy networks, mutual socialising.'
29   According to a GMBU union press office release, 11 June 1996.
30   D Gordon, op cit, p42.
31   Both studies quoted and analysed in ibid, p39.
32   For an account of his views, see S Flanders, 'Developing Countries Call the
      Tune', *Financial Times*, 6 October 1995.
33   Quoted in W Ruigrok and R van Tulder, op cit, p138.
34   Ibid, p218.
35   Ibid, p219.
36   Ibid, p219.
37   J Stopford and S Strange, op cit.
38   Ibid.
39   Quoted in the *Financial Times*, 20 June 1988.
40   J Stopford and S Strange, op cit.
41   W Ruigrok and R van Tulder, op cit, pp157-158.
42   Ibid, pp157-158.
43   Ibid, pp161-163.
44   *Financial Times*, 3 August 1996.
45   M Mann, op cit, p120.
46   Ibid.
47   For an account of this period, see my book, *Explaining the Crisis*, op cit, chapters
      2-3.
48   M Mann, op cit, p119.
49   See R C O Matthews, 'Why Has Britain Had Full Employment Since the War?',
      Economic Journal, September 1968, p556.
50   As I wrote in 1976: 'The era in which the state could protect national capitalists
      from the direct impact of world crisis is drawing to an end... Each national state

capitalism is more and more sucked into a chaotic, disorganised world system where the only order is that provided by the crises and destructiveness of the world market itself'. 'Poland and the crisis of state capitalism', *International Socialism* (first series), 93 and 94.

51   Quoted in R Skidelsky, *John Maynard Keynes*, vol 2 (London, 1994), p378.
52   R Hilferding, letter to Karl Kautsky, 2 October 1931, quoted in P F Wagner, *Rudolf Hilferding, Theory and Politics of Democratic Socialism* (New Jersey, 1986), p155.
53   Ibid.
54   W Ruigrok and R van Tulder, op cit, p284.
55   The most recent figures, for 1993, show that foreign owned companies were responsible for 25 percent of manufacturing output, and 35 of the 100 largest manufacturing companies were foreign owned (up from 18 in 1986). Half of big foreign owned businesses were from the US (unchanged since 1986), 39 percent from Europe (more than double the 1986 figure), but only 7 percent from Japan or Korea, despite the enormous media publicity for these. *Financial Times*, 4 September 1996.

Marxism and sport

CHRIS BAMBERY

Sport is enjoyed by millions of people in our society—and also, precisely for the same reason, sport is big business. Total revenues generated by sport in the US and Canada (from ticket sales to purchases of sports equipment) were more than $88.5 billion dollars last year, and are projected to rise to $160 billion by the turn of century. It is estimated that by then North American firms would be spending $13.8 billion dollars on advertising through sport alone—while global sports advertising is set to reach $430 billion. The television rights to the US National Football League for 1990-1994 earned NFL $43.6 billion. Nike's total sales in the US were $4.73 billion in 1994. Some $600 million came through Michael Jordan branded basketball shoes! In 1993 Nike spent almost $90 million on advertising and marketing.

Football is often touted as the 'people's game'. Yet for many, attendance at a premiership game is simply beyond their means—that's if they can get a ticket to see big clubs like Manchester United or Newcastle United. The Chelsea versus Aston Villa game at the beginning of the 1996-1997 season saw each of the 28,000 people attending pay, on average, £20 a head. For the 1,750 away supporters who were permitted access there was no concession for children—they also paid £20. This perhaps helps explain why the *Social Trends* survey shows that while 22 percent of the UK population attended a sports event as a spectator, more still are listed as having visited a historic building (23 percent), the cinema (33 percent) or the library (39 percent).[1] The survey also shows that in Britain 'people in social class AB were twice as likely to have gone swimming or played in team sports than those in social class E'.[2]

For some clubs the money collected at the gate is no longer the key element in their finances. *The Guardian* on 14 September 1996 carried a report on the finances of England's biggest club, Manchester United:

> *Of United's £60 million turnover last season, £23 came from one, surprising source: merchandising—everything from replica shirts and videos to books and bedside lamps. To put £23 million in perspective, we are talking a figure larger than the entire annual turnover of any premiership club except Newcastle. To give an idea of volume, United's magazine is, at 140,000 copies, the biggest selling sports monthly in the UK. In Thailand it sells 40,000 copies a month—in Thai. Its first print in Norwegian last month sold out 9,000 copies in a week. Soon it will be sold in Malaysia in Malay.*

Income from satellite television alone means that England's Premier League clubs will take in £670 million between 1996 and 2001.[3]

The most recent high point for English football was the hosting of Euro 96 and the home nation's achievement in reaching the semi-final (where they were only knocked out in the second stage of a penalty shootout). At the England-Germany semi-final there were 14,000 people who paid nothing for their tickets as a result of corporate hospitality—3,500 tickets were given to sponsors, while 7,000 plus were sold through corporate hospitality.[4] The cost of such hospitality by big business was worth a total of £8 million for the whole tournament. The next football World Cup will be in South Korea and Japan. Japanese multinationals have already established a close relationship with FIFA, the competition's organiser: 'JVC, Fuji and Canon each sponsored USA 94 to the tune of £20 million, Sony Creative Products have exclusive marketing rights to the 1998 finals and Dentsu control a 49 percent stake in ISL Worldwide, the marketing arm of FIFA'.[5] This is the direct and easily recognised relationship between sport and capitalism. But there is another, hidden relationship.

As England progressed towards the semi-finals of Euro 96 the *Financial Times* carried the following survey of big business reaction to the supposed euphoria sweeping the nation:

> *Jeff Forest of Sheffield based Tempered Spring reported: 'The England performance has given people a lift, and a happy workforce is a better workforce.' Mr Peter Lowe who manages an automotive plant in Burton-on-Trent, subsidiary of Johnson Controls, 'believes that a run of England victories will lead to higher productivity'.[6]*

If we move beyond the most obvious links between capitalism and sport and ask why it is that millions of people watch sport we must begin with the work process and the reality of alienation under capitalism— just as the capitalists quoted by the *Financial Times* look to the effect of sport on the work process. For the vast majority of people sport is something they enjoy. It is an essential escape mechanism in their lives. For some it can become the means of clambering out of poverty. For others participation in sport gives dignity to life. For millions of people sport seems to provide an escape from the drudgery of everyday life. For many more watching sport either live or, increasingly, on television provides both a release from workday pressure and an easy identification with an individual, club or country which seems to provide meaning to life. As one veteran follower of West Ham remembers, football provided 'relief from work, from war...it was a way out. In the late 1920s the times were very hard'.[7]

It is against the reality of work—not just in a factory but in a modern office, school or hospital—that we can examine the role of 'leisure' under capitalism. Marx points out, 'At the same time that factory work exhausts the nervous system to the uttermost, it does so with the many-sided play of the muscles, and confiscates every atom of freedom, both in bodily and intellectual activity'.[8] Elsewhere he wrote, 'Time is everything, man is nothing; he is, at most, time's carcass'.[9]

In *Labour and Monopoly Capital* Harry Braverman argues, 'In a society where labour power is purchased and sold, working time becomes sharply and antagonistically divided from non-working time, and the worker places an extraordinary value upon this "free" time, while on-the-job time is regarded as lost and wasted...'[10] Everyone has heard people say, 'Thank God it's Friday,' or has hung around waiting to clock off. The weekend, or whatever time we get off, is 'our time'—it is 'free time'.

Leisure is seen as something distinct from work, something to be earned as recompense for a 'fair day's work'. The Polish Marxist Franz Jakubowski writes, 'The alienation of labour has the effect of an alienation of man from man. Social life becomes merely a means for man's self-preservation'.[11] Consequently, 'free time' is not really 'our time' either. Braverman develops the point:

> But the atrophy of community and the sharp division from the natural environment leaves a void when it comes to the 'free' hours. Thus the filling of the time away from the job also becomes dependent on the market, which develops to an enormous degree those passive amusements, entertainments, and spectacles that suit the restricted circumstances of the city and are offered as substitutes for life itself. Since they become the means of filling all

the hours of 'free' time, they flow profusely from corporate institutions which
have transformed every means of entertainment and 'sport' into a production
process for the enlargement of capital...

Braverman adds, 'So enterprising is capital that even where the effort
is made by one or another section to find a way to nature, sport or art
through personal activity and amateur or "underground" innovation,
these activities are rapidly incorporated into the market so far is
possible'.[12]

Let's look at some of the ways in which capitalism commodifies and
distorts the desire for escape and real, human contact which draws
people to sport in the first place.

For instance, one of the often quoted enjoyments of attending a football game is being part of the crowd. Yet at its best the 'mateyness' of the
crowd is a substitute for the genuine fraternal feelings of human beings.
Those feelings can only be fully developed by liberated human beings
who are themselves free, autonomous individuals (and we would argue
the way to achieve such a society is through the collective struggle of the
working class).

Sport, despite the perception of participants and spectators, belongs to
the realm of 'unfree activity'. The rationality of capitalist production,
based on commodity exchange, reduces all individuality to a minimum.
It organises and controls people not only in their work but in their
leisure. Adorno writes, 'Amusement in advanced capitalism is the extension of work. It is sought after by those who wish to escape the
mechanised work process, in order to be able to face it again.' Adorno
points out that the promise of sport is the liberation of the body humili-
ated by economic interests, the return to the body of a part of the
functions of which it has been deprived by industrial society. 'Sport
restores to mankind some of the functions which the machine has taken
away from him, but only to regiment him remorselessly in the service of
the machine'.[13]

Even the human body suffers under the pressure exerted on individuals to be the 'right' shape. The images of what is supposed to be human
beauty are displayed before us daily. For many the desperate search for
the 'right' shape results in pain and misery. The reality is that perceptions about our bodies are socially constructed. They are given meaning
by social relations. For much of human history fatness was to be welcomed because it signified wealth in a world of hunger. Perceptions of
'beauty' have changed through the ages as even a brief examination of
Renaissance paintings will reveal.

Capitalist competition affects every kind of human activity—intruding
into love, play and all social relations. In sport obsessive repetition—who
can run fastest, who is the strongest, who can throw furthest—increases

the alienation of the individual. Sports ideology, like all ideologies, conceals the real structure of productive and social relations under capitalism. These are of course seen as 'natural'. Relations between individual humans within the sporting institutions are transformed into material relations between things: scores, machines and records. In the process human bodies are treated as commodities.

Ideology would have us believe that sportsmen and women are free and equal. This then justifies them being ranked into different grades. The hero of this ideology is the 'self made' man or woman who attains their advancement on the basis of their own merit and through their own efforts. The lesson is that anyone can make it to the top. The reality is rather different. The teenagers who become professional footballers are not necessarily the 'best' or most talented players. They are often those most prepared to accept the tight discipline and intensive training demanded of them.

Let two managers of top football teams who are usually portrayed as representing two different traditions of play—one swashbuckling and attacking, the other dour and defensive—speak for themselves. Tottenham Hotspur manager Bill Nicholson explained that when seeking new players what he looked at above all was 'character': 'Training is vital, repeating and repeating every possible action... I prefer players not to be too good or clever at other things. It means they concentrate on football.' He is echoed by Bertie Mee of Arsenal: 'We are basically concerned with winning matches and that means scoring goals. Some players may be exciting to watch but, in the end, product is what matters. I want a high level of consistency—a man who can produce it in 35 games out of 42.'

In the spring of 1996 Vincent Hanna wrote in *The Guardian*:

> *Suppose someone told you there was a regime in Europe where agents scoured the country looking for talented young boys, who are taken from their homes and brought to camps to do menial jobs and train constantly—for whom, because of the intense competition for places, education is cursory. The lucky ones are kept on, bound under a contract system where they can be bought and sold by employers. The successful and the bright do very well. But many of the second raters will find themselves, in their 30s, on the scrap heap and unemployed.*

In any other industry this would raise howls of protest. Yet, as the author notes, 'thus does Britain produce "the greatest football league in the world".'[14]

Discipline and training in modern sport often equals a massive distortion of the human body which can lead to all sorts of horrors. The pressure and the money involved in top class football in Britain have in recent months produced stories headlining three England internationals' alcohol problems, and two of those refer to involvement in fairly horrendous domestic abuse. In these cases it is not an exaggeration to say that in the pursuit of success the notion of childhood has been destroyed.

In a powerful indictment of the world of women's gymnastics and figure skating, Joan Ryan reports:

> *What I found was a story about legal, even celebrated child abuse. In the dark troughs along the road to the Olympics lay the bodies of girls who stumbled on the way, broken by the work, pressure and humiliation. I found a girl whose father left the family when she quit gymnastics at the age of 13, who scraped her arms and legs with razors to dull her emotional pain and who needed a two-hour pass from a psychiatric hospital to attend her high-school graduation. Girls who broke their necks and backs. One who so desperately sought the perfect, weightless gymnastic body that she starved herself to death. Others—many—who became so obsessive about controlling their weight that they lost control of themselves instead, falling into the potentially fatal cycle of bingeing on food, then purging by vomiting or taking laxatives. One who was sexually abused by her coach and one who was sodomised for four years by the father of a teammate. I found a girl who felt such shame at not making the Olympic team that she slit her wrists. A skater who underwent plastic surgery when a judge said her nose was distracting. A father who handed custody of his daughter over to her coach so she could keep skating. A coach who fed his gymnasts so little that federation officials had to smuggle food into their hotel rooms. A mother who hid her child's chicken pox with make-up so she could compete. Coaches who motivated their athletes by calling them imbeciles, idiots, pigs, cows.*[14]

Ryan goes on to chart the changes in modern women's gymnastics:

> *In 1956 the top two Olympic female gymnasts were 35 and 29 years old. In 1968 gold medalist Vera Caslavska of Czechoslovakia was 26 years old, stood 5 feet 3 inches and weighed 121 pounds (eight stone and nine pounds). Back then, gymnastics was truly a woman's sport. It was transformed in 1972 when Olga Korbut—17 years old, 4 feet 11 inches, 85 pounds (six stone and one pound)—enchanted the world with her pigtails and rubber-band body. Four years later 14 year old Nadia Comaneci clutched a baby doll after scoring the first perfect 10.0 in Olympic history. She was 5 feet tall and weighed 85 pounds (6 stone 1 pound).*
>
> *The decline in age among American gymnasts since Comaneci's victory is startling. In 1976 the six US Olympic gymnasts were, on average, 17 and a half years old, stood 5 feet three and a half inches and weighed 106 pounds*

(seven stone and eight pounds). By the 1992 Olympics in Barcelona, the average US Olympic gymnast was 16 years old, stood 4 feet 9 inches and weighed 83 pounds (five stone and thirteen pounds)—a year younger, 6 inches shorter and 23 pounds lighter than her counterparts of 16 years before.[16]

From these observations we can conclude that sport is characterised by: (a) competition—trying to be first, beating an opponent or to do better than others (setting a new record); (b) the notion of record as central—this reflects a society where everything is measurable and quantifiable; (c) sporting scales of value which are precise, very hierarchical and obvious to all; (d) training—which is the hard labour of sport. Training is increasingly inhumane, based on techniques very similar to the production line and involving the same inhumane workpace.

Yet for all the obvious parallels between these characteristics and the broad values of capitalism and workplace relations, the connection between capitalism and sport is commonly rejected. Sport is seen as a timeless thing, something 'as old as the hills'. Yet for the majority of the time human beings have been on the planet they have not known anything approximating to modern sport. Primitive societies, on the contrary, saw humans co-operate together to eke out an existence. Physical exercise was part of day to day reality rather than something separated from the work process.

Competitive sport emerged with the development of class societies in which a privileged minority—either a military or religious caste—controlled the surplus produced by agricultural societies. It is, of course, possible to draw links and comparisons with what might be termed sport in previous societies. But the function they played in those societies was very different from modern sport and bears little real resemblance to the activities we describe as sport today.

The ancient Greeks are credited with being the first organisers of sport on a systematic basis—the Olympic Games which began in 776 AD are often cited as evidence of this. But Cashman points out:

The games may have been less important as a spectacle than they were as a focal point around which to organise training. Physical fitness, strength and the general toughness that derives from competition were important military attributes, and so the process was tuned to producing warriors as much as sports performers.[17]

The Olympics originated as part of a religious festival dedicated to Zeus. The games were only open to a privileged minority—they excluded slaves and women. The games were closely associated with the development of the state, with warfare between the states, and with the state internally having a monopoly of violence:

> *Powerful Greek city-states needed defence against outside attacks and they ensured this by encouraging and rewarding warriors. Accompanying the development of the **polis** was the growth of the state's control over human expressions of violence; sophisticated social organisation and internal security were impossible without some regulation of violence. The state's response was to obtain a legitimate monopoly over violence and establish norms of behaviour which discouraged the open expression of violence by citizens and encouraged saving violence for the possible repulsion of attacks from outside powers. Contests, challenges, and rivalries were ways in which the impulse could reassert itself, but in socially acceptable forms.*[18]

In both ancient China and Japan there was activity with a ball. *When Saturday Comes* recently carried an article on a form of 'keepy up'—*kemari*—traditionally played by Japanese aristocrats. It was 'seen as a sign of breeding, ball control a measure of social prestige'. It remains so among the 30 ageing Japanese who still 'play' it. It is, however, not competitive. It is played in a costume dating from the 6th century and, after the players kneel as a mark of respect to the ball, the game continues with the ball being simply passed among the participating males using headers and volleys. The whole thing seems to be a form of meditation tied to Buddhist ritual—rather different to modern soccer.[19]

In other societies sport played a similar role. Among Native Americans lacrosse was often played across several days as a form of ritualised or substitute warfare.[20] Medieval and pre-industrial ball 'games' in Britain, usually played with an inflated pig's bladder, were often melees rather than games. Those that have continued into the present day suggest they were about demarcation of boundaries between or in villages with little distinction being made between spectators and participants. They were conducted according to custom rather than by fixed rules. There is no obvious connection between these events and modern games like football and rugby. Even on the eve of the industrial revolution the work process was largely dictated by the agricultural seasons while artisans still retained a degree of control over the work process. There was time for festivals and play, the maypole being one of the better known examples. As the process of primitive capital accumulation began climaxing in the industrial revolution these were ruthlessly stamped out. Historians like Christopher Hill and E P Thompson provide a rich history of opposition to this process.

Notions of play and physical exercise have changed throughout history. How could it be otherwise? Many of the institutions that are portrayed today as timeless are in fact a product of systems of production

whose role and character have changed as ancient society was replaced
by feudalism and as feudalism was replaced by capitalism. The Catholic
Church is a good case in point. Marx criticises those 'who fail to see our
social institutions as historical products and understand neither their
origin nor their development'.[21] In *The German Ideology* the point is
developed: 'All common institutions are set up with the help of the state
and are given a political form'.[22]

Football lays claim to being the most popular game in today's world.
Yet its origins lie in the 'muscular Christianity' of England's mid-19th
century public schools. Their aim was to turn out 'great men' in a system
based on the survival of the fittest. Soccer was codified by ex-public
school boys, the first written rules were drawn up at Cambridge
University in 1848, and public school educated men controlled the
Football Association when it was formed in 1863. The original FA Cup
winners included Wanderers, Royal Engineers, Oxford University, Old
Etonians, Old Carthusians. This domination by the public schools was
only breached in 1878 when a professional team, Darwen, first appeared
in an FA Cup final. From then on professional teams with working class
players dominated the sport.

When it was a public school/Oxbridge sport, football was played by
young men whose future careers were as bankers, captains of industry or
administrators of empire. They required a high degree of autonomy, initiative and self discipline. The emphasis then was on individual dribbling
skills. In the very first days of football, prior to 1850, there were no specialised positions. The first functional division was between defence and
attack. Then the goalkeeper acquired a specialised role. Even the 1863
rules contain no mention of a goalkeeper—that first appears in revised
rules of 1870. Today dribbling plays a very subordinate role in any major
team. Ryan Giggs, for instance, will often be in direct contact with the
ball for only 15 seconds during a normal 90 minute game.

British football evolved into a traditional pattern of the long ball game or
short stabbing passing movements which stemmed from the need to play on
waterlogged pitches in mid-winter! But it is the technical conditions of the
factory and work, which determine behaviour at the workplace, which have
increasingly been reproduced on the playing field by systems of play and
tactical manoeuvres to which players are supposed to subordinate themselves.

Football developed in the second half of the 19th century after industrial production had stabilised from the years earlier in the century when
men, women and children were expected to work long hours in often
appalling conditions. Industrial production required skill—and that
required a healthy and relatively content workforce. Saturday afternoon
holidays opened the way for popular sport. A quarter of the Football

League's clubs were founded by the churches keen to grow in the new urban working class areas: Aston Villa grew from a men's bible class, Birmingham City from Holy Trinity Church, Bolton from Christ Church, Everton from St Domingo's Congregational Church Sunday school.

Industrialists too were quick to see the advantages of sport. Arsenal was formed from workers at the Royal Arsenal in Woolwich. Other clubs whose origins lie in works teams include West Ham United (Thames Iron Works), Manchester United (Lancashire & Yorkshire Railway), and Southampton (Woolston shipyard), while Sheffield Cutlers became Sheffield United. Professionalism was made legal in 1885 after years in which it had been tacitly accepted. This spread of sport into the working class from above was central to the creation of a 'respectable' working class following the upheavals of the post-Napoleonic and Chartist years.[23]

Football was quickly spread across the globe by British engineers, soldiers, factory owners and missionaries (witness Anglicised names like Newells Old Boys in Buenos Areas and AC Milan in Italy). But though soccer may have been played by workers, it was always as a professional game controlled and directed by the upper classes.

Capital by the mid-19 century was shifting away from the methods of exploitation associated with the industrial revolution. It increasingly required a skilled or semi-skilled workforce provided with a modicum of education, health provision and 'rest'. The employers were not slow to see how these could be used to discipline the working class. Looking back to this period, Ellis Cashman writes:

> *Behaviour at work was subject to rules and conditions of service. Usually all the work took place in a physically bounded space, the factory. There was also a need for absoluteness: tools and machines were made to fine toler-ances. Underlying all this was a class structure, or hierarchy, in which some strata had attributes suited to ruling and others to being ruled. The latter's shortcomings were so apparent that no detailed investigation of the causes was thought necessary: their poverty, or even destitution, was their own fault.*
>
> *All these had counterparts in the developing sports scene. Time periods for contests were established and measured accurately thanks to newer sophisti-cated timepieces. Divisions of labour in team games yielded role-specific positions and particular, as opposed to general, skills. Constitutions were drawn up to instil more structure into activities and regulate events according to rules. They took place on pitches, in rings, in halls—infinite spaces. Winners and losers were unambiguously clear, outright and absolute. And hierarchies reflecting the class structure were integrated into many activities.* [24]

Given its origins—and particularly the spread of games like soccer, cricket and baseball which came with the rise of imperialism—the connection between sport and nationalism has always been close. The Turner Movement, the championing of a system of gymnastics and physical exercises devised by Friedrich Jahn, was associated with the creation of German national unity against Napoleonic occupation. Jahn argued that gymnastics was about 'protecting youth from softness and excess in order to keep them sturdy for the coming struggle for the fatherland'. Official schools' gymnastic manuals of 1862 and 1868 prescribe exercises modelled on Prussian military drill regulations of 1847. Marching in ranks and columns, turning on the march, wheeling, division into sections, etc were to be practiced under the eye of the gymnastics teacher. These moves were bitterly opposed by the German socialists.

Modern imperialism means more than extending the influence of capitalists from the major powers overseas. It also means sinking deeper roots among the working class at home so that they can be mobilised behind the imperial project. The development of modern sport coincided with the extension of the franchise, a key stage in this process. In 1866 a Tory government under Disraeli took the 'leap in the dark' by extending the franchise for the first time to workers—though still on a very restricted basis. Prior to then, parliamentary politics at Westminster had essentially been restricted to a small number of ruling class patricians. From 1866 the Tories began to build themselves into a mass membership party. The ruling class had to develop new ideological tools to establish control over the masses. In Britain this would have included the development of the popular press with the launch of the *Daily Mail*.

This coincided with the rise of imperialism. Imperialism was not only a question of the subjection of the colonial populations. For Lenin and other Marxists imperialism was important as a means of ideologically tying the masses to their own ruling class through the ideas of nationalism and racism. Organised sport originated in the imperialist nations—they drew up the rules and formed the governing bodies in the years between 1860 and 1890. C L R James in *Beyond a Boundary* shows how cricket was used in the British West Indies to disseminate ideas central to maintaining colonial rule across British colonies. Cricket was spread across Britain's empire just as US imperialism ensured baseball became the national sport of Cuba, Puerto Rico, Mexico and much of Central America.

An examination of when modern sport was regulated and codified gives some evidence of its link to modern industrial capitalism and the state. In fact the process of regulation was closely associated with the rise of imperialism. The Football Association was founded in 1863; Rugby Union in 1871 (Rugby League split in 1895). Across the Atlantic Baseball's National League was founded in 1876. Three years afterwards six day cycle races began in Europe. The invention of the modern

Olympic Games by Baron Pierre de Coubertin—the first games were held in Athens in 1896—owed something to the English public school tradition but flowed rather more directly from the Franco-Prussian War. Coubertin was convinced after visiting England that Arnold's methods at Rugby school had been part of the rise of British power in the 19th century and that these had to be transplanted to France. Coubertin also saw physical health as being necessary to win wars. If France was to overcome its defeat in the Franco-Prussian War physical education had to become central to the education system.

In the imperialist countries sport played an important role in bolstering a nationalism which had previously often had only a tenuous hold on popular consciousness. The Tour de France helped create the idea of a French nation state just as football in Italy became a symbol of an Italian nationalism which, prior to the First World War, had been extremely fragile.

Under dictatorships we can see the naked role of sport in our society and its clear connection to nationalism. The 1936 Berlin Olympics were the first to be televised. The games themselves were transformed into a mass propaganda event. Today the 1936 games are best remembered for the slap in the face that the black American athlete Jesse Owen gave Nazism by winning four gold medals. But the impact of Hitler's propaganda should not be ignored. One Uruguayan journalist recalled: 'Everything was organised towards a political end...to show a brilliant Germany... Their effort was a triumph for them because people left enchanted with the country and the treatment they had received'.[25]

Of course the claim is often made that bringing athletes together promotes peace. In his history of the Olympics, *Olympic Politics*, Christopher R Hill points out:

> *If this is taken to mean that athletic competition promotes a camaraderie which inhibits hostility there is not much evidence to support it in top level sport. High level sport is now so closely linked with large sums of hard cash that there is little room for friendship, and investigation of the idea that interaction on the sports field produces friendly feelings has shown that the thesis is by no means necessarily true, at any level.*

He then points out,

> [that] *nearly every celebration of the* [Olympic] *Games has been marked by acrimony or worse and the recollections of contretemps or disaster long outlive the warm glow of competitive interaction. A catalogue would be tedious, but it is worth remembering that other Games than those held in Berlin in 1936 have provoked international outrage. For example, 1968 saw*

a massacre by the Mexican government of young people who thought the Games a waste of money. Israeli athletes were murdered by Palestinians at the Munich Games of 1972 when the outgoing President of the International Olympic Committee, Avery Brundage, decided that 'The Games must go on'. In 1976 numerous African states boycotted the Games in protest against a rugby tour of South Africa undertaken by a New Zealand side.[26]

Since then that catalogue has continued with the next Olympic games in Moscow witnessing a boycott over the Russian invasion of Afghanistan.

The same pattern is also observable in other international sports events. The first World Cup final played in Montevideo in 1930 saw the Uruguayan home side come from 2-0 down against Argentina to win the tournament 4-2. In the city that night the home supporters rejoiced. But across the border, 'in Buenos Aires, the defeated Argentinians raged; mobs took to the streets, even stoning the Uruguayan consulate, and diplomatic relations between the countries were broken off'.[27]

Sport then is totally integrated into a framework of inter-state rivalry, capitalist production and class relations. As an ideology, transmitted on a huge scale by the media, it is part and parcel of ruling bourgeois ideology. The hierarchical structure of sport reflects the social structure of capitalism and its system of competitive selection, promotion, hierarchy and social advancement. The driving forces in sport—performance, competitiveness, records—are mirrors of the driving forces of capitalist production.

John Hargreaves argues that organised sport helps train a 'docile labour force' with the discipline necessary for modern capitalism. Comparing sport and industry, he notes 'a high degree of specialisation and standardisation, bureaucratised and hierarchical administration, long term planning, increased reliance on science and technology, a drive for maximum productivity and, above all, the alienation of both producer and consumer'.[28] He adds that 'sport is produced, packaged and sold like any other commodity on the market for mass consumption at enormous profits'.[29] And he argues that sport expresses in a concentrated form bourgeois ideology (aggressive individualism, ruthless competitiveness, elitism, chauvinism, sexism and racism) and that its bureaucratic administration is linked closely to the capitalist state.

But Hargreaves is aware that by concentrating large numbers of people together capitalism can create the conditions in which disorder and opposition can grow. Commenting on the crowd he argues, 'It is precisely this type of solidarity that historically has formed the basis for a trenchant opposition to employers'.[30]

Recently the police have opened fire on a football crowd in Libya, killing many people, after they began chanting opposition to the regime of Colonel Gadaffi. In Spain under Franco hatred of Real Madrid and support for Barcelona could both signal opposition to the regime. There have also been examples of participants using sporting occasions to make a political protest. The most potent was by the two black Americans who finished first and second in the 200 metres at the 1968 Olympics. As they stood on the podium, and as the national anthem was played, both raised a fist in the black power salute (and both were barred from athletics as a result).

Socialists should have no qualms about supporting any such manifestations. From its inception the Anti Nazi League sought sponsorship from sports personalities and campaigned against racism on the football terraces. That campaign helped spawn a number of local initiatives at football clubs, often linked to fanzines. In 1996 this all culminated in the launch of a 'Let's Kick Racism Out Of Football' campaign sponsored by the Commission for Racial Equality and the Professional Footballers Association.

Yet we should be careful about exaggerating the general importance of these examples. The main anger of a football crowd is directed against the opposing players and their supporters. That anger can take the form of the worst kinds of verbal abuse, and sometimes of physical violence.

In Britain, recent years have seen a number of rebellions against the boards of directors at a number of football clubs. Yet this too has its contradictions. At Tottenham Hotspur the ousting of the manager and director, Terry Venables, by the club's owner, millionaire Alan Sugar, saw a number of protests on Venables' behalf by Spurs fans. Yet it is hard to see either figure as representing the fans' best interests. At Celtic in Glasgow a highly successful campaign by fans succeeded in ousting the old Catholic middle class families who had run the club since its inception and whose lack of vision and investment had seen the club trail their rivals, Rangers. Yet many Celtic fans must have experienced the strange sensation of knowing that what was really necessary was for the club to be taken over by someone, or some multinational, which could give an even bigger injection of cash than Rangers had received in order to create success on the field. That, of course, would inevitably entail the club following others in promoting overpriced merchandising and introducing seat prices which would prohibit most working class fans from attending matches with any regularity. Competition has its own logic.

Sport without competition, on and off the field, is a contradiction in terms. It is a tyranny over human effort by machines, the watch, and arbitrary rules. This is as true of 'team' sports as of 'individual' sports. Some argue sport can be about competing against oneself—as if Robinson Crusoe his on desert island were to try to set a new record for running round the island or for outswimming a shark! But such arguments are not only entirely implausible, they also miss the point. The main point goes to the fundamental question of human nature and of socialism. In sport the element of *play* has increasingly disappeared. Ellul argues:

> We are witnessing a process whereby playfulness and joy, contact with air and water, improvisation and spontaneity, are disappearing: all these things are abandoned in favour of obedience to strict rules, efficiency and record times. Training turns men and children into efficient machines who know no other joy other than the grim satisfaction of mastering and exploiting their own bodies.[31]

Former Spurs captain Mike England, in Hunter Davies's *The Glory Game*, states: 'I never say I'm going to play football. It's work.' No one was *playing* in Euro 96, the Olympics or at the last World Cup.

Socialists want to rescue the element of play in leisure. Capitalism creates a large class of people engaged in sedentary labour who need physical activity as a diversion. And it creates a specialisation of labour where even those engaged in physical labour develop only those physical attributes which are useful for production. Socialism will abolish this set-up and create the conditions for the free development of the human body. Under socialism there will be physical recreation—but not sport.

Sport does not equal all physical activity. Sport is one way of being physically active. But it is increasingly an artificial means of achieving fitness. The result in professional (and increasingly amateur) sport often becomes the physical distortion of the human body in pursuit of a record. Take this example:

> June 18 1994, the body of 22 year old Russian, Aleksandr Popov, breaks the water of a pool at Monaco, Monte Carlo. Moments later, Popov fully surfaces, having travelled 100 meters through water faster than any other human. In 48.21 seconds, Popov has set in motion processes and mechanisms of immense complexity: for 61 strokes, his every muscle contracted, stretched and twisted; his lungs have filled and emptied repeatedly; his heart has pumped about 6.6 gallons (30 litres) of blood into all areas of the body.[32]

In order to achieve this new record Popov had reduced his body to an intricate machine. At what cost? Who will remember him in ten or 20 years time? What will a 42 year old Aleksandr be like?

Brohm talks of 'the total, not to say *totalitarian mobilisation* of the athletes to produce maximum performance. Every sport now involves a fantastic *manipulation of human robots* by doctors, psychologists, bio-chemists and trainers. The "manufacturing of champions" is no longer a craft but an industry, calling on specialised laboratories, research institutes, training camps and experimental sports centres'.[33] Taking drugs to enhance performance, far from being a new phenomenon arose at the same time as professional sport came to be used as an expression of newly minted imperial rivalries:

> *...after 1879 when six day cycle races began in Europe, riders favoured ether and caffeine to delay the onset of fatigue sensations. Sprint cyclists used nitroglycerine, a chemical later used in conjunction with heroin, cocaine, strychnine, and others to make 'speedballs' which were given to racehorses before races in the 1930s. The highly poisonous strychnine was also used by the winner of the 1904 Olympic marathon.*[34]

There is not a qualitative difference between using drugs to artificially enhance performance and the physical abuse inflicted on the body by other means.

There are of course certain contradictory elements in sport—witness popular opposition to the police among football crowds. At best these are an inarticulate and misdirected protest against capitalism. But even these are rare. Even the love of being in a crowd reflects the atomisation and lack of community we suffer under capitalism, a pale reflection of what real human solidarity would be like. The buzz, the excitement, comes because people see it as a break from the mundane reality of everyday life. But the buzz goes quickly and it *isn't* a break from capitalist reality.

Trotsky once had occasion to refer to how the creative potential of working class people is caricatured by popular pastimes. Writing on Britain, Trotsky points out, 'The revolution will inevitably awaken in the English working class the most unusual passions, which have been hitherto been so artificially held down and turned aside, with the aid of social training, the church, the press, in the artificial channels of boxing, football, racing and other sports'.[35] Elsewhere he adds, 'In the sphere of philanthropy, amusements and sports, the bourgeoisie and the church are incomparatively stronger than we are. We cannot tear away the working class youth from them except by means of the socialist programme and revolutionary action'.[36]

The one attempt at starting to construct a socialist society took place in the terrible conditions of post First World War Russia. It was strangled at birth by Stalinist counter-revolution. Yet the debates which occupied the Bolsheviks retain their relevance. Trotsky, in *Problems Of Everyday Life*, attempted to deal with the issue of creating not just a new society but new men and women. There is little or no mention of sport because in the primitive stage of Russian society this scarcely existed for the Russian working class. Nevertheless, there are three points which have some bearing on sport:

(1) *The question of amusements in this connection becomes of greatly enhanced importance in regard to culture and education. The character of the child is revealed and formed in its play. The character of an adult is clearly manifested in his play and amusements... The longing for amusement, distraction, sightseeing and laughter is the most legitimate desire of human nature. We are able, and indeed obliged, to give the satisfaction of this desire a higher artistic quality, at the same time making amusement a weapon of collective education...* [37]

(2) *Everyone knows that physical requirements are very much more limited than spiritual ones. An excessive gratification of physical requirements quickly leads to satiety. Spiritual requirements, however, know no frontiers. But in order that spiritual requirements may flourish it is necessary that physical requirements be fully satisfied.* [38]

(3) *...meaningless ritual, which lies on the consciousness like an inert burden, cannot be destroyed by criticism alone; it can be supplanted by new forms of life, new amusements, new and more cultured theatres.* [39]

The case for socialism rests on the idea that humans can be co-operative not competitive. Pre-class societies abound with such examples. The French paper *Socialisme Internationale* recently told of Jacques Meunier's description of a game played by the Morés Indians in Amazonia: 'The player who scores automatically changes team. In that way the winners are weakened and those who are losing are reinforced. The score equalises in this way'. [40]

In a socialist society we will not be alienated—from work, from leisure, from nature. Indeed the divisions between these things would cease to exist. For the first time we would have 'the right to be lazy' . William Morris subtitled *News From Nowhere* an 'Epoch of Rest' in which we would be free to enjoy 'the light of the world'. It would be a world in which there are endless possibilities. Most people prefer swimming in a warm sea to a chlorine saturated swimming pool. Interestingly, swimming in the sea is fun, because people indulge in play, rather than in trying to outdo each other. In contrast swimming pools are increasingly laned-off and extremely competitive, intimidating people who want a leisurely swim up and down and making it impossible for a family or a group of friends to play.

Socialism will not be a society where 22 men still play football (far less where another 30,000 people will pay to watch them) or men and women crash up and down a swimming pool competing against each other and the clock. Physical recreation and play are about the enjoyment of one's body, human company and the environment. Sport is not. It is about competing, doing better than the next person, being the best. It is about obeying arbitrary rules—an ideal preparation for the capitalist productive process.

Naturally socialists understand why people take part in or watch sport. It is an escape from the harsh world in which we live. That is why we do not ignore sport. Rather socialists campaign, for instance, against racism on the terraces and seek the support of sports men and women for such campaigns. Neither would socialists dream of banning or prohibiting participation in sports. But socialists should follow the example of the Bolsheviks in pulling out of all sports competitions based on nationalism, such as the Olympics. Our aim is human liberation and a world of truly endless possibilities, a world in which future generations will look back in wonder at something like the Olympics and ask only one question—Why?

Notes

1   *Social Trends* 25 (HMSO, 1995), p220.
2   Ibid, p224.
3   *The Independent*, 16 September 1996.
4   *The Guardian*, 26 June 1996.
5   *When Saturday Comes*, May 1996.
6   *Financial Times*, 26 June 1996.
7   G Hodgson, *The People's Century* (BBC Books, 1995), p128.
8   K Marx, *Capital* vol I (Lawrence and Wishart, 1974), p398.
9   K Marx, 'The Poverty of Philosophy'in *Marx and Engels Collected Works* Vol VI (Lawrence and Wishart, 1975), p127.
10   H Braverman, *Labour and Monopoly Capitalism* (Monthly Review Press, 1974), p278.
11   F Jakubowski, *Ideology and Superstructure in Historical Materialism* (Pluto Press, 1990), p86.
12   H Braverman, op cit, pp278-279.
13   Quoted in J-M Brohm, *Sport: A Prison of Measured Time* (Pluto Press, 1989), p56.
14   *The Guardian*, 8 May 1996.
15   J Ryan, *Little Girls in Pretty Boxes* (Women's Press, 1996), pp3-4.
16   Ibid, p58.
17   E Cashman, *Making Sense of Sports* (Routledge, 1996), p60.
18   Ibid, pp60-61.
19   *When Saturday Comes*, May 1996.
20   See *The Guardian*'s Notes and Queries column, 11 September 1996.
21   K Marx, 'Letter to P Annenkov, 1846', in *Marx and Engels' Selected Works* (Lawrence and Wishart, 1970), p663.
22   K Marx and F Engels, *The German Ideology* (Progress Publishers, 1976), p99.
23   J Hargreaves, *Sport, Power and Ideology* (Routledge Kegan and Paul, 1982).
24   E Cashman, op cit, p73.
25   G Hodgson, op cit, p144.
26   C R Hill, *Olympic Politics* (Manchester University Press, 1992), pp35-36.
27   G Hodgson, op cit, p123.
28   J Hargreaves, op cit, p41.
29   Ibid, p41.
30   Ibid, p110.

31   Quoted in J-M Brohm, op cit, p41.
32   E Cashman, op cit, p23.
33   J-M Brohm, op cit, p18.
34   E Cashman, op cit, p145.
35   L Trotsky, *Writings On Britain* vol II (New Park, 1974), p123.
36   L Trotsky, *Whither France* (Pathfinder Press, 1968), p102.
37   L Trotsky, *Problems of Everyday Life* (Pathfinder Press, 1994), p32.
38   Ibid, p24.
39   Ibid, p34.
40   *Socialisme International* 104, 19 June-3 July 1996.

Computers and consciousness: a reply to Alex Callinicos

JOHN PARRINGTON

Alex Callinicos gives an excellent description of the revolutionary significance of Darwin's theory of natural selection in his review of Daniel Dennett's new book, *Darwin's Dangerous Idea* in *International Socialism* 71. However, while Alex is not uncritical of Dennett, pointing out some of the major flaws in his acceptance of sociobiology, I was surprised to discover no such criticism of what must be one of Dennett's core ideas—the notion that the human mind can be compared to a computer.

Alex tells us that Dennett has been:

> concerned to develop what might be described as a non-reductionist materialist theory of the mind. In other words, he has sought to find a way of treating the mind as a natural phenomenon, whose activities are continuous with those in the physical world, while at the same time recognising that human beings are 'intentional systems' whose behaviour cannot be explained without ascribing to them beliefs, desires and other mental states.[1]

I find such a statement hard to accept given that Dennett's computer model of the mind is one of the primary forms of reductionism operating in psychology today.[2] According to this viewpoint, consciousness is an emergent property that appears whenever brains achieve the right degree of complexity. But a brain, according to the same school of thought, is just a machine that carries out computational processes. Computers, just like brains, could achieve consciousness, and we would have to regard the conscious self, in Dennett's own words, as merely 'the programme that runs on your brain's computer'.[3]

There are a number of fundamental flaws in such an approach. Firstly, there is the assumption that we can ignore the physical differences between brains and computers. Alex expresses this in his statement that 'mental activity is best understood less in terms of the physical hardware it depends on (the brain and nervous system in humans), but rather in terms of the functions which it realises'.[4] Sussex University philosopher Margaret Boden put it rather more bluntly in her claim that 'you don't need brains to be brainy'.[5]

Yet a straightforward comparison between the respective structures of brains and computers shows this assumption to be completely wrong. A crucial difference is that of determinacy. The units (chips, AND/OR gates, logic circuits, etc) of which a computer is composed are determinate, with a small number of inputs and outputs, and the processes that they carry out with such impressive regularity are linear and error free. They can store and transmit information according to set rules.[6]

Such determinacy is a necessary thing if computers are to work effectively. Imagine how you would feel if, when you punched in 'quit' onto a computer terminal, the computer instead displayed next week's engagements—or printed your last file, not always, just when it felt like it. If you couldn't debug that programme, you would junk it right away.

Brains, however, are not constrained by such rigid determinism. As Steven Rose explains:

> *The brain/computer metaphor fails because the neuronal systems that comprise the brain, unlike a computer, are radically indeterminate... Unlike computers, brains are not error-free machines and they do not work in a linear mode—or even a mode simply reducible to a small number of hidden layers. Central nervous system neurons each have many thousands of inputs (synapses) of varying weights and origins... The brain shows a great deal of plasticity—that is, capacity to modify its structures, chemistry, physiology and output—in response to contingencies of development and experience, yet also manifests redundancy and an extraordinary resilience of functionally appropriate output despite injury and insult.[7]*

If such features are a general property of animal brains, a qualitatively different level of complexity and indeterminacy is found in the human brain. Human beings are fundamentally different from animals in a number of important respects.[8] One is our ability to act upon and change the world around us by using hands and tools.[9] But another crucial difference is the fact that we are the only species that possesses the linked capacities of reason, reflection and self conscious awareness.[10] Animals can feel pain, hunger, contentment etc, but only we are conscious that we feel these things.

Understanding the nature of human consciousness is obviously a fundamental problem for psychology. Dennett is quite right to reject the approach of Descartes, who saw consciousness as some metaphysical essence within the material brain, the homunculus (little man) in our heads lording it over the rest of us.[11] But there is another way of understanding human consciousness which does not have to resort to such idealist notions. First put forward by the Marxist psychologist Lev Vygotsky in the 1920s and most recently by the American psycho-linguist Derek Bickerton, this alternative approach stresses the central role of language in structuring our minds.[12]

The distinctive feature about human language, as opposed to the sounds and gestures made by animals, is that we use words to refer to things and situations that are not actually present in front of us. We use them to abstract and generalise from the reality that confronts us and to describe other realities. But once we can do this to others, we can also do it to ourselves, using the 'inner speech' that goes on inside our heads to envisage new situations and new goals. Thus language creates the material basis for consciousness within the brain, without recourse to any of the internal homunculus Descartes envisaged.

It should be stressed that, while consciousness is based on language, they are not identical.[13] Unlike animals, we have the ability to reflect and reason, but we still share with animals our biological needs and our emotional responses which must also play a part in our thought processes.[14] Neither is the development of consciousness a passive process. It has been shown that children actively seek out the words and concepts that make sense of their everyday practical experience.[15] What is more, 'inner speech' itself appears to be a dialogue, reflecting opposing ideological perspectives drawn from society as a whole.[16]

It is this unique synthesis between the social element expressed in language and the individual element expressed in biological and emotional needs that makes human consciousness not only distinct from that of animals, but also something that would be impossible to replicate within a computer. Dennett's claim that human consciousness can be compared to a computer rests on his assumption that computers are intentional systems, presumably meaning they possess 'beliefs, desires and other mental states'[17] like us. But surely this is just confusing the intentionality of the machine with that of its maker.[18] Our intentionality as human individuals stems from a self conscious awareness of what our actions mean both within the context of society and in our interactions with other human beings. It is this infusion of human consciousness with meaning that introduces a further level of indeterminacy into our consciousness that is lacking in computers.[19] Computers are oblivious to the meaning of what they are doing—they merely process the information they are given according to the instructions of a set programme.

One way to illustrate the vast difference between humans and computers is to look at the question of memory. Computers, we are told, are similar to humans because they have 'memories' in which they store information. It is sometimes even suggested that computers have superior memories to us because they do not forget things. In fact computer memory is no more like human memory than the teeth of a saw are like human teeth. To describe both as memory is to use loose metaphors that embrace more differences than similarities.[20] Computers 'remember' things as discrete entities. Each item is separable, perhaps designated by a unique address or file name, and all of it subject to total recall. Unless the machine malfunctions, it can regurgitate everything it has stored as exactly as it was entered, whether a single number or a lengthy document. That is what we expect of a machine.[21]

In contrast to this, the items of information that the human memory recalls are not selected as isolated units but by their meaning within the wider whole of consciousness. And because we inhabit a biological shell, memory can also involve the emotions, the senses, etc. One of the best descriptions I have read of the strange dynamics of human memory comes not from a scientist, but from the author Vladimir Nabokov:

> *A passerby whistles a tune at the exact moment that you notice the reflection of a branch in a puddle which in turn and simultaneously recalls a combination of damp leaves and excited birds in some old garden, and the old friend, long dead, suddenly steps out of the past, smiling and closing his dripping umbrella. The whole thing lasts one radiant second and the motion of impressions and images is so swift that you cannot check the exact laws which attend their recognition, formation and fusion... It is like a jigsaw puzzle that instantly comes together in your brain with the brain itself unable to observe how and why the pieces fit, and you experience a shuddering sensation of wild magic.*[22]

On a more mundane level, the importance of meaning for human memory is illustrated by the fact that in laboratory experiments, if given meaningless bits of information to remember, people can only remember 7 ± 2 items.[23] Obviously not on a par with most pocket calculators, never mind a computer. However, ask a Socialist Workers Party district organiser for members' phone numbers, or a football supporter for the day's scores (as in the experiment above), and they will undoubtedly be able to remember a good deal more!

I believe the flaws in Dennett's computer model of the mind also help to explain why such an undoubtedly sophisticated thinker ends up supporting such a crude model of cultural evolution as sociobiologist Richard Dawkins's theory of memes.[24] As Alex points out in his review, memes are an entirely idealist notion brought in to offset the crude mechanical materialism of sociobiology.[25] As such they tell us nothing about where ideas come from. But if we look at the properties of memes, described by Alex as a hopeless jumble of different categories functioning in isolation from each other, isn't this a good description of the way we find information stored on a computer? Of course, the separate files on a computer are linked together in a different way—that is, in the head of the person who put them there.[26] Viewed in this way, Dennett's enthusiasm for the concept of memes becomes not so much an anomaly as a logical extension of his computer model of the mind.

Finally, what relevance does all of this have for socialists? Firstly, I think we should be very sceptical of much of the hype surrounding Artificial Intelligence (AI).[27] From its origins in the Second World War[28] there has always been an intense military interest in AI. This reached a crescendo during the 1980s under the auspices of Ronald Reagan's infamous Star Wars programme but the interest continues to this day. As Steven Rose has observed: 'It has become hard these days to attend a scientific conference on themes associated with learning, memory and computer models thereof, without finding a strongly hovering US military presence'.[29] The result is that AI has been one of the most richly funded fields of academic research over the last few decades.

In order to justify the billions of dollars invested in AI, it is important for its backers to be able to point to something more inspiring than the production of bigger and better weapons of mass destruction. So in 1958 Allen Newell and Herbert Simon, two of AI's founding fathers, were predicting that we would soon have computers with problem solving powers 'coextensive with the range to which the human mind had been applied'.[30]

By 1970 no such machines had materialised, but that didn't stop AI guru Marvin Minsky[31] from declaring:

In from three to eight years, we will have a machine with the general intelligence of an average human being. I mean a machine that will be able to read Shakespeare, grease a car, play office politics, tell a joke, have a fight. At that point, the machine will begin to educate itself with fantastic speed. In a few months, it will be at genius level, and a few months after that, its power will be incalculable.[32]

Needless to say, the point at which this day of reckoning will occur has successively been pushed back with each passing decade.

If all this sounds like an outsider sniping, it is worth noting that a significant part of the criticism of AI has come from within the computer community itself. Some researchers are worried that the alliance between information technology and the Pentagon is distorting the priorities of the research. But more basically still, there are those who argue that AI has been oversold to a degree that flirts with outright fraud.[33] So it was an IBM employee, Lewis M Branscomb, who observed that, with respect to AI, 'the extravagant statements of the past few years have become a source of concern to many of us who have seen excessive claims by researchers in other fields lead to unreasonable expectations in the public'.[34] The charge was put even more pointedly by Herbert Grosch, formerly of IBM: 'The emperor—whether talking about the fifth generation or AI—is stark naked from the ankles up'.[35]

The point is not to denigrate the enormous advances which have been made in computer science but to be rather more realistic about the limits of what computers will and will not be able to do compared to human beings in the coming decades. This is an important political point given continual reports in the media about how computers will soon be putting us all out of our jobs.[36]

The fact is, computers are only superior to human beings in those areas where we might expect them to be: that is, in those areas where rapid processing power and monotonous, regular and error free behaviour are called for. So in my own line of work—genetics—it is much quicker to use a computer to scan DNA sequences than to do it manually (and much less monotonous for me!). Computers have also excelled at chess playing, a rule based game where rapid computational skills are an asset.[37]

However, when we turn to what may seem to humans as much simpler tasks requiring only 'common sense', it is precisely there that computers' limitations have most visibly emerged. So computer scientists are still struggling to develop a robot system which can pile an orange pyramid onto a blue cube,[38] or follow a simple set of instructions relating to everyday life.[39] And given what we have said about the importance of language in human consciousness, it is significant that no computer has yet been able to successfully translate languages—one of the first skills predicted by AI theorists.

The second problem with AI is the very negative influence it has had on psychology. Given that psychological theories inform debates on social matters as diverse as the question of working mothers, the treatment of prisoners, school testing and crowd control,[40] socialists have an interest in the development of progressive theories of the mind and cannot ignore reactionary ones. The mainstream form of psychology until recently was behaviourism.[41] This is the idea that human behaviour can be explained as nothing more than learned responses to outside stimuli. Pavlov's dogs became the accepted model for human behaviour. As a theory of the mind behaviourism was not only crude, mechanical and wrong—it also had some extremely reactionary practical consequences. Sensory deprivation, restricted diet, solitary confinement and loss of remission for prisoners, the pin down methods used in children's homes, even the idea that it is right to smack children, all come from behaviourism and the idea that people can be trained like animals.[42]

Since the 1960s there has been a reaction in psychology against the crudest ideas of behaviourism—this is the so called 'cognitive revolution'.[43] Initially the new cognitive psychology looked as though it was going to be a great improvement on behaviourism. For the first time in years psychologists were talking about consciousness, meaning and social context, not just about nerve reflexes. But, despite a promising start, cognitive psychology has turned out to be largely a dead end. The reason was the full scale adoption of the mind as computer model. One of the consequences is that mainstream psychology today is full of flow charts which have a distinct resemblance to computer diagrams. Uncertainties or 'woolly' concepts like context or background are often relegated to single input boxes (with an arrow feeding in, for example, cultural factors).

The result is that cognitive psychology has turned out to be as incapable as behaviourism of explaining how and why people behave as they do. As Huddersfield University psychologist Nicky Hayes puts it:

> *Cognitive psychology has sold itself, and the rest of psychology, short. It has failed to provide the alternative which was so badly needed after the dominance of behaviourism. The cognitive obsession with the computer metaphor meant that it fell into the same trap for which it criticised the behaviourists. By defining the human being using a metaphor, and then taking the metaphor as if that were the only possible reality, it rendered itself unable to respond to the real issues and challenges which were being thrown up.[44]*

In summary, the problem with comparing human consciousness to a computer is that it is based on a gross underestimation of what it means to be human. Computers process information and so do humans, but, whereas that is all that computers do, information processing is only one side of human consciousness. The other side, and the side that also distinguishes us from animals, is that for humans all information is also infused with meaning.

So how does the confusion over what should be obvious differences between ourselves and computers occur? After all, it is not only AI theorists who believe computers will soon be able to do everything a human can—many ordinary people are worried about whether computers might one day take their jobs. I think it has a lot to do with what Marx called our alienation from society under capitalism. According to Marx's theory,[45] workers are alienated from capitalist society not simply because most don't feel happy and satisfied with that society, but literally, because they have no control over their work and what happens to the things they produce. Under capitalism everything is defined as a commodity, not by how useful it is. So an expensive car can become an unattainable object of desire. Products can appear to have a life of their own, or, as Marx put it, they become a fetish object, despite the fact that they were once made by ordinary workers. With computers, because superficially they can seem to have characteristics similar to our own minds, this fetishisation seems to have gone one step further—machines that we make can nevertheless be seen as a threat to our jobs and potentially as our future masters. This peculiar reversal of roles could only occur in the upside down world of capitalism. In a socialist society we will be able to properly view and utilise computers for what they are—fantastically advanced tools, but tools nonetheless.

Notes

1   A Callinicos, *International Socialism* 71, p101.
2   N Hayes, *Psychology in Perspective* (Macmillan, 1995), ch 8 pp109-114.
3   D C Dennett, *Consciousness Explained* (Boston, 1991), p430.
4   A Callinicos, op cit, p101.
5   M Boden, in S Rose and L Appignanesi (ed), *The Limits of Science* (Blackwell, 1986).
6   S Rose, *The Making of Memory* (Bantam, 1992), p88.
7   Ibid, p89.
8   J Parrington, 'What makes us human?' Tape of talk at Marxism 96 available from Bookmarks.
9   F Engels, 'The Role of Labour in the Transition from Ape to Man', in *Dialectics of Nature* (Progress, 1954), pp170-183; C Harman, *International Socialism* 65, pp83-142.
10 As long ago as Aristotle, humans have been defined as reasoning animals, but the distinction is developed most recently in D Bickerton *Language and Human Behaviour* (UCL, 1996).
11 D C Dennett, op cit, p313.
12 L Vygotsky, *Thought and Language* (MIT, 1986); D Bickerton, op cit. Note that, while Bickerton's analysis complements the Marxist one, there are problems with his approach which will be tackled in my forthcoming *International Socialism* article on the Russian philosopher, Voloshinov.
13 Developed in L Vygotsky, op cit, ch 7, pp210-256. Note that inner speech itself has a different, much more fluid structure from spoken language, leaving space for a great deal more flexibility than the latter.
14 Though it is important to realise that even the most 'natural' of our urges, such as hunger or the sexual urge, are also intimately linked to social values.

15   L Vygotsky, op cit, Chapters 5 and 6, pp96-209.

16   V Voloshinov, *Marxism and the Philosophy of Language* (Harvard, 1973).

17   A Callinicos, op cit, p101.

18   Derek Bickerton classifies Dennett as a victim of CAP syndrome (computer assisted pygmalionism). Pygmalion was the legendary Greek sculptor who carved a statue so beautiful that he immediately fell in love with it. To be able to do this he presumably had to believe that he and the statue were organisms of a similar kind. D Bickerton, op cit, pp123-124.

19   Ibid, p151.

20   The phenomenon is particularly prevalent in sociobiology with regard to animal versus human behaviour.

21   T Roszak, *The Cult of Information* (Paladin, 1988), p116.

22   V Nabokov, 'The Art of Literature and Common Sense', in *Lectures on Literature* (Harcourt Brace Jovanovich, 1980).

23   P E Morris et al, *British Journal of Psychology*, 72, pp479-483.

24   R Dawkins, *The Selfish Gene* (Oxford University, 1989).

25   A Callinicos, op cit, pp109-111.

26   I think Dennett's idea of sub- or pseudo-intentionality as a lower level of consciousness arises from this source too.

27   T Roszak, op cit, is best for a general account.

28   Through the need to develop effective servo-mechanical devices to calculate elevation and direction so as to fire anti-aircraft guns against rapidly moving targets techniques developed by the US mathematician Norbert Weiner, who gave the new science a new name, cybernetics.

29   S Rose, op cit, p79.

30   Quoted in T Roszak, op cit, p144.

31   Minsky's influence on Dennett is apparent in his eclectic set of 'categories of mind' which sound very similar to Dennett's memes. See M Minsky, *The Society of Mind* (Simon and Schuster, 1985).

32   Quoted in T Roszak, op cit, pp144-145.

33   Ibid, p146.

34   Quoted in ibid, p146.

35   Ibid, p146.

36   Not that one should ever be complacent about the threat to some jobs because of increasing automisation—the point is that the extent and success to which computers can replace workers are often exaggerated for political purposes.

37   R Penrose, *The Emperor's New Mind* (Vintage, 1989), pp16-17. Penrose, however, notes that computers 'play' chess in quite a different way from humans, going rapidly through every possible move, whereas humans use much more judgment to select alternatives.

38   S Rose, op cit, p91.

39   T Roszak, op cit, p147.

40   N Hayes, op cit. Also J Parrington, 'Marxism and Psychology'. Tape of talk at Marxism 96 available from Bookmarks.

41   N Hayes, op cit, ch 2, pp19-33.

42   The classic satire of behaviourism—the film *Clockwork Orange*—may have seemed shocking, but the real life practical consequences are almost as bad, as documented in Rose, Kamin and Lewontin's *Not in Our Genes* (Pelican, 1984), pp175-178.

43   N Hayes, op cit, ch 8, pp105-121.

44   Ibid, pp120-121.

45   A Callinicos, *The Revolutionary Ideas of Karl Marx* (Bookmarks, 1995), ch 4, pp65-81.

Dennett, materialism and empiricism

JOE FAITH

Alex Callinicos is absolutely correct to recommend Daniel Dennett's writings on the mind and evolution.[1] Dennett gives clear introductions to exciting areas of science and philosophy. Moreover he is a consistent materialist, and socialists always have something to learn from them. However, he belongs to a very different philosophical tradition to classical Marxism. Callinicos mentions this in passing, but neither identifies the root of the difference nor what effects it has.

Cause and correlation

The underlying problem is with how we understand cause in the natural world. Dennett, along with Richard Dawkins and the vast majority of other practising scientists, is an empiricist. This means that he ultimately agrees with David Hume's definition of cause as simply being a correlation between events: if you find that whenever A happens, then B follows, and that if A doesn't then B doesn't, then this is what we mean by A causing B. For example, if you flick a switch, then the light comes on. If you don't then it won't. If this is the case then *by definition* the switch caused the light to come on. Richard Dawkins is quite explicit in his agreement—at least in how the concept of 'cause' is used in practice:

> *Philosophers, possibly with justification, make heavy weather of the concept of causation, but to a working biologist causation is a rather simple statistical*

*concept. Operationally we can never demonstrate that a particular observed event C caused a particular result R, although it will often be judged highly likely. What biologists in practice usually do is to establish **statistically** that events of class R reliably follow events of class C... Statistical methods are designed to help us assess, to any specified level of probabilistic confidence, whether the results we obtain really indicate a causal relationship.*[2]

Dennett, being a philosopher, is never going to be tied down that simply, but he too basically agrees: 'If one finds a predictive pattern of the sort just described one has *ipso facto* discovered a causal power—a difference in the world that makes a subsequent difference testable by standard empirical methods of variable manipulation.'

The problem with this definition of cause is that it doesn't give us a way of looking beneath the surface appearances of events, to their underlying reality. Marx once noted that if the world worked just as it appeared to, then there would be no need for science. Only when we understand the processes going on beneath the surface can we understand how the situation can change. Take a simple example. Most people who bought a council house during the 1980s voted Tory in 1987; most who refused, or couldn't afford to, didn't. The empiricist must draw the conclusion that buying a council house causes voting Tory. There is certainly an element of truth in this, but we all know that the real situation is far more complicated. A specific economic and political situation, including rising property prices, caused both house buying and Tory voting. Therefore they were correlated. If the situation changes, for example, if falling house prices produce negative equity, then the link between house ownership and voting intentions changes. These days it is those trapped with big mortgages compared to their income who most want to strangle Major. The empiricist definition of cause raises a correlation between events into a real mechanism, and tends to obscure the complexities and dynamics of real life.[4] You can see why it has always been the favourite philosophy of the British ruling class.

The empiricist definition of cause tends to mix up the processes of *description* and *explanation*. A description of a series of events just picks out significant regularities in them. An explanation, on the other hand, starts from a description, then relates these regularities to forces and mechanisms that are not present in the data described, but rather go on beneath the surface. We only know a description is correct if we can 'ground' it in an explanation.

For example, before Darwin discovered natural selection, many biologists agreed that species evolved; they just argued about the mechanism that caused it. The most widely held theory was Lamarck's. He believed that organisms passed on characteristics that they developed during their life—for example, baby giraffes would have long necks because their parents had to stretch theirs in order to reach leaves on trees. This theory was fairly adequate at describing the biological data at the time and certainly as adequate as Darwin's theory. In fact, natural selection seemed to contradict two known facts. The first was that it would have meant evolution worked incredibly slowly—it would have taken longer than then known age of the earth. It also required characteristics of organisms to be passed on in an all or nothing fashion, when any child of a tall and a short parent knows that they tend to get averaged out. Natural selection wasn't generally accepted until the start of the century, when the work of Mendel on genetics was rediscovered. Genetics provided an underlying mechanism for natural selection that resolved the problems of how characteristics get passed on. Until then the two theories fitted the known data equally well. According to an empiricist, they would be equally true. It is only once we look beneath the surface that we can see which one describes a real process.

Surface appearances are not comprised of unarguable facts, but are shaped by current theories. For example, the age of the earth was calculated from the rate at which objects cool down and the earth's current temperature—in the same way that you can tell how long a pie has been out of the oven by how hot it is. It was later discovered that the earth *generates* heat, and so it would have taken longer to cool down. The age of the earth was recalculated as 4.6 billion years, and there was found to be enough time for evolution through natural selection to take place. Darwin was right *despite* (some of) the then known facts.

The status of intentionality

This argument about cause has implications for our understanding of the mind. Callinicos is completely uncritical of Dennett's notion of intentionality—the property of our thoughts that they are *about* something external to us. Intentionality is assumed every time we describe someone (including ourselves) as thinking *that* so and so is the case, or wishing *that* such and such would happen. This might all sound too obvious for words, but it isn't. Many cultures throughout history have ascribed intentionality to all sorts of things—winds, trees, rivers—that we wouldn't want to. Others would explain human actions, not in intentional terms like beliefs and desires, but in terms of spirits, humours, the hand of God, and so on. The philosophy of phenomenology makes a practice of trying to eliminate rational intentionality from explanations of human behaviour. The question is, how do we know we are right, and that these other explanations are wrong? Postmodern philosophers would argue that we can't claim that our interpretation is any more correct, and that they are all just different ways of looking at the world.

Do we have any better answer than this?

If we are to be consistent materialists, then we have to assume that intentionality is something to do with the way our brains and bodies work, and their relationship to the things that we think about. To put it at its most crude, what makes our thoughts of a cat *about* a cat (rather than just being a purely private, internal, affair)? The simple answer is that our thoughts can cause our bodies to reach out and grab a cat, and so bring our thoughts into contact with their contents through our actions. Of course we have as yet very little idea about how all this works,[5] but we have to assume, as Engels did, that some kind of explanation is possible. This does not imply that mental phenomena will some day be reduced to the physical, but that some kind of relationship can be found. Until we find such a causal explanatory link, then our intentional descriptions remain just that, descriptions. And like any description unsupported by an understanding of the underlying mechanism, like Lamarck's description of evolution, they are susceptible to being found incorrect.

Dennett would disagree fundamentally with this. According to him, what makes intentionality real (what he calls 'being a true believer') is not its potential to be united with the rest of science, but rather just the fact that it works. If we describe people's behaviour using beliefs and desires (what Dennett calls 'taking the intentional stance'), then we can make incredibly accurate predictions. I can talk to someone on the phone and arrange to meet them somewhere. I could then predict that they would leave their house, that they would pick up an umbrella if it was raining, what route they would walk, what they would do if they had to cross a road and there was a car coming, and so on. All this belief and desire knowledge is very good at describing what people do, and for Dennett this means that it is true: when we say that someone believes something, all we actually mean is that it is useful to suppose that they believe it: '...all there is to *really and truly believing that p is being an intentional system for which p occurs as a belief in the best (most predictive) interpretation*'.[6] In other words, intentionality is a real, material, causal property simply because it is a very good description. This is the old empiricist equation of correlation and cause. This is dangerous. The ancient Greeks managed to build huge military and political empires, for which they needed a *very* good predictive description of human intentional behaviour. According to Dennett this would make their theory of humours and spirits as 'true' as our scientific approach. Does Callinicos really want to allow this?

This also has implications for how we think about artificial intelligence computer systems. For example programs called 'expert systems' have been written that can answer questions about, for example, cats.

They can tell you what they look like, what they eat, how long they live, and so on. If it was a person answering the questions you would be convinced that they had a pretty good idea of what a cat was. But a cat could leap on top of the computer and it wouldn't know anything about it; the computer's knowledge exists in a form completely separated from the material world. Nonetheless, because the computer gives such a convincing impression of someone who knows what they talking about, then Callinicos is forced to follow Dennett in saying that it has real beliefs, even though it is completely cut off from the world that it is supposed to know about. This is a version of *dualism*—the claim that ideas are not part of the material world—and is something that Marxists have fought long and hard against.

Dennett and evolution

Having failed to identify the real disagreements between Dennett and ourselves, Callinicos seems almost surprised when Dennett turns out to agree with the theory of the 'selfish gene'. He shouldn't be, since it is a direct consequence of Dennett's empiricist view of cause. The heart of the selfish gene theory is what Francis Crick (who co-discovered the structure of DNA) calls the 'central dogma of biochemistry'. This states that every aspect of the physiology and behaviour of the organism that carries them (called *traits*) is caused by particular genes. Since traits affect how successful the organism is at reproducing—and so passing on its genes to the next generation—then natural selection is really a competition between genes to survive. It is this theory that allows the theory's best known advocate, Richard Dawkins (and Dennett), to describe organisms (including humans) as lumbering robots programmed by our selfish genes.

Now it is true that changes in particular genes are correlated with changes in traits. Moreover, the chances of the organism successfully reproducing, and so passing on its genes to the next generation, are correlated with these traits. According to an empiricist this means that a specific gene *caused* a specific trait, and that the specific trait *caused* the gene to spread. Given this simple causal picture you can have an account of natural selection that doesn't even mention organisms, just genes.[7] The real picture is far more complex. Traits are properties of organisms that are produced by a process of development. This process is the product of the interaction of the organism with its genes and the natural and social environment. We have to understand how all these things combine if we are to understand biology and human culture, just as we had to understand the forces underlying council house buying and Tory voting.

I have also got a couple of niggles about Callinicos's account of natural selection. The basic problem is that he sees natural selection as being about the evolution of organisms adapted to given conditions. However, this ignores the fact that it is the products of evolution that themselves determine (albeit unconciously) what those conditions will be. As Lewontin puts it, organisms are the objects and subjects of evolution—they construct their own environment.

As a result Callinicos gives a one sided picture of natural selection being primarily about competition for resources. It is equally true to say that evolution favours organisms that *avoid* competition. Fighting is very expensive; it is usually better to find ways to co-operate. Species such as flies, rats and humans are successful because of their flexibility in locating alternative resources, compared to butterflies, squirrels and chimps.[8] Instead of competing for a given set of resources, they find a new environment.

This also has implications for our understanding of determinism in evolutionary histories. Stephen Jay Gould claims that, if the tape of evolution were rewound and allowed to unfold again, then it could look very different. Callinicos, following Dennett, argues that, since both versions face the same initial conditions, then they are bound to follow similar paths. Once we understand that organisms define their own conditions, then the variability in the initial population can quickly lead to very divergent histories. Although this might seem like a purely abstract argument, we can in fact test it in practice. It is now possible to reproduce a form of natural selection in computer simulations, called 'artificial evolution'. Even with the incredibly simple environments and organisms being simulated today, it is possible to see very different results from repeated evolutionary 'runs'. Natural selection isn't about finding optimal solutions to given problems. Organisms define their own problems and solutions simultaneously.

Conclusion

Times are tough for materialist philosophers of mind; and when times are tough, you can't be too choosy about your friends. Nonetheless this doesn't mean that you should be unclear about, or bury, your differences. The differences between Dennett and the tradition of this journal are not incidental; they are deep. But I hope that won't stop anyone reading his books.

Notes

Thanks to Helen Crudgington for many useful discussions. The author is a researcher in the School of Cognitive and Computing Systems at the University of Sussex.

1   A Callinicos, 'Darwin, Materialism and Evolution: a Review of Daniel Dennett's *"Darwin's Dangerous Idea".' International Socialism* 71.

2   R Dawkins, *The Extended Phenotype* (W H Freeman, 1982), p12.

3   D C Dennett, 'Real Patterns', *The Journal of Philosophy*, 88 (3), (1991), p45.

4   For more on empiricism, materialism and cause, see A Collier, *Critical Realism: An Introduction to the Philosophy of Roy Bhaskar* (Verso, 1994). Bhaskar's original writings are incredibly hard to follow, and often almost mystical, but the first half of this book is a very good defence of the idea that science can break through surface appearances to understand underlying causes.

5   But for a good introduction to what we do know, see S P R Rose, *The Making Of Memory* (Bantam, 1992).

6   D C Dennett, *The Intentional Stance* (MIT Press, 1987), p29.

7   This issue is dealt with more fully by the great Marxist biologist Richard Lewontin in 'Artifact, Cause and Genic Selection', *Philosophy of Science* 49, 1982, pp157-180.

8   For more on how competition is understood, see 'Competition: Current Usages', in E F Keller and E A Lloyd, *Keywords in Evolutionary Biology* (Harvard University Press, 1992).

Who made the American Revolution?

*A review of Theodore Draper, **A Struggle for Power: the American Revolution** (Little Brown, 1996), £25*

MEGAN TRUDELL

The Declaration of Independence was signed 220 years ago, marking the triumph of America's first bourgeois revolution and the defeat of the world's foremost imperial power at the time, Britain. Famously, the language of the declaration asserted the importance of liberty and rights: 'We hold these truths to be self evident, that all men are created equal, that they are endowed by their creator with certain unalienable rights, that among these are life, liberty and the pursuit of happiness.'[1]

These rights, which would be more clearly spelt out in the Bill of Rights—the first ten amendments to the Constitution—in December 1791, were of central importance to the rule of the bourgeoisie. They sprang from the way in which it had waged its revolution, and contained its more radical elements: freedom of religion, freedom of the press, the right to peaceable assembly, the right of people to bear arms, and, crucially, the security and protection of property. These would in turn be adopted and extended by the French bourgeoisie in the course of the French Revolution. They represented a great step forward from absolutism, though they did not eradicate real social or economic inequality.

We are taught, in as much as we are taught about it at all, that the American Revolution was a purely political event in which the few founding fathers, guided by these high principles, fought a 'tidy little war'[2] which left the existing class structure intact. Textbooks generally agree that the revolution's 'main significance was unquestionably political'.[3] The American Revolution is thus reduced to an avoidable squabble.

Even *The Guardian's* Edward Pearce in a review of Draper's book argues that the 'colonies might have been kept longer to be relinquished without conflict'.[4]

The revolution did raise the banner of liberty through democratic slogans of the rights of man, and representation, but it had its roots in deep contradictions between Britain and the colonies and was marked by violent struggles, not polite confrontation. The revolution was both a fight against British rule and a struggle for power between different forces on the American side. It paved the way for dramatic economic and social change.

'The American Revolution shattered the old colonial system'.[5] It was more than simply an exchange of control between Britain and the emergent American ruling class. It transformed the colonies from mere extensions of British markets overseas into a unified country with a vigorous manufacturing base in the North. It set the stage for enormous expansion westwards—which did not simply involve the heroic pioneering West of the myth, but also the systematic expulsion from the land of the native American population and their eventual extermination—and the growth of large scale slavery in the South. The revolution eliminated the rule of British officials, royal governors, and the semi-feudal land arrangements which included passing titles down through families. It freed the capitalist class in America to embark unfettered on the capitalist road.

The revolution provided the state institutions necessary to give maximum encouragement to merchants' interests—developing commerce, the free market, trade and the development of manufactures. The expansion of farming to the West and the spread of the plantation system initially served the bourgeoisie, who bought raw materials and supplied finished goods. It was not until the 1860s that the clash between the North's industrial revolution and the South's slave economy, still tied to Britain, resulted in the vast and bloody second stage of America's bourgeois revolution—the American Civil War.

Against the standard view, Theodore Draper's book argues that the clash between Britain and the American colonies was inevitable—the clash between an existing empire and a rising economic power. He points to 'a "real cause" that "made war inevitable"—the growth of the power of the Americans, and the alarm this inspired in Great Britain.'[6] Draper moves away from the interpretations of the revolution as purely about ideological struggle, and concentrates on 'a struggle for power—between the power the British wished to exercise over the Americans and the power the Americans wished to exercise over themselves'.[7]

Draper's study traces the causes of the revolution back to the colonial arrangement with Britain. It takes us in great detail through the growing tensions that ultimately led to the colonies uniting to force the break with their imperial master, researched from many contemporary pamphlets and the letters of British officials from both sides of the Atlantic as well as, to a lesser extent, the writings of leading colonists.

Britain and the colonies

Britain was already a powerful nation by the 1770s. The defeat of France in the Seven Years War meant Britain was not only the world's greatest naval power, but was also pre-eminent in European trade with Africa and Asia. Especially important was the 'triangular' trade of slaves, staples like sugar, tobacco and tea, and manufactured goods between Britain, North America and the West Indies. Trade aided the growth of investment in manufacturing—mainly metals and woollens—as well as shipping and shipbuilding. Though Britain's industrial base was growing, the explosion of growth of the industrial revolution was still a few years off and at this stage Britain was building up and protecting its burgeoning industry.

From Britain's point of view, its colonies were there to provide the raw materials essential to British manufacture and to provide sure markets for finished British goods. The Navigation Acts enacted after the English Revolution ensured that all colonial trade was carried in English ships with English crews. Certain 'enumerated' goods that were especially important to Britain as raw materials (tobacco, furs and indigo among them) had to be traded via London, unloading and paying duties before continuing on to their ultimate destination. The colonies were not permitted to be traded between themselves, or to issue paper money. The Molasses Act of 1733 aimed at cutting colonies' trade with France by slapping 100 percent duty on non-British sugar.

Although a lot of these restrictions were avoided through widespread smuggling—allowing New England especially to build up a rapidly growing and profitable trade in molasses, rum and slaves with France and the West Indies—the relationship with Britain was still heavily weighted towards the imperial power.

The revolution would be led by a coalition of two classes—the emergent Northern bourgeoisie and the large scale planters of the Southern colonies. To understand the reasons why these people, many made wealthy by the relationship with Britain, would be in the forefront of the struggle that would sever that relationship, we have to look at the economic and social relations within and between the different colonies. Unfortunately Draper's study does not give the fullest picture of these relations.

The American colonies of the 1760s and 1770s were not a unified state, but a loose collection of 13 provinces, with a combined population of only 3 million. They were economically weak, certainly in comparison with

Britain. They had separate histories and no tradition of acting together.

What, if anything, united the different colonies was a shared notion of Britishness, that America was part of a free nation in an age of absolutist monarchy. This was an important identification that was to prove easier for some to break than others. Even the political parties in America reflected those in Britain—Tories, loyal to the crown and to British rule, and Whigs, the British parliamentary opposition to the Tories and forerunners of the Liberal Party.

Ninety percent of colonists worked the land, producing crops for export. The Southern colonies produced vast amounts of staple goods on increasingly large plantations—tobacco in Virginia and Maryland, rice and indigo in South Carolina and Georgia. The plantation system rested on slavery, which provided labour and helped to bind whites to the planters and offset any chances of united revolt.

Plantation owners produced for the world market but all their produce was marketed by the British, who handled three quarters of all the Southern trade in their ships, compared to New England which handled three quarters of its trade in American ships. Thomas Jefferson, who was to become one of the sharpest revolutionary minds, and a Virginia planter himself, described the relationship:

> They [British merchants] *reduced the prices given him for his tobacco, so that…they never permitted him to clear off his debt. These debts had become hereditary from father to son for many generations, so that the planters were a species of property annexed to certain mercantile houses in London.*[8]

It is little wonder that the majority of planters were firmly anti-British throughout the revolutionary period, while those small farmers and the poor ruled over by rich planters in the South were often loyal to the crown. The colonists were by no means united in their opposition to Britain, a factor Draper does not discuss.

The merchants in the North were the other key force, though generally subject to greater pulls towards loyalism and compromise than the planters. New England was predominantly commercial, with growing industry that was linked to trade. In the North agriculture was based mainly on small farmers, some with tenancies held by big landlowners—who were overwhelmingly Tories loyal to the crown and defenders of British rule. Both the landed aristocracy and the merchants in the towns would divide into Tory and patriot wings during the revolution.

The merchant class in the towns prospered within the colonial system and from trade with the South. Shipbuilding boomed and, as part of the reciprocal trade, the colonies had the protection of the British navy for goods in transit as well as sure markets in Britain. This meant the merchants would, in the course of the struggle against Britain, be the section most likely to vacillate and to stave off separation.

The possibility of economic independence was already present by the 1760s. As Draper makes clear, America was a dynamic society—between 1720 and 1750 the colonies' population more than doubled, exports nearly doubled, and imports more than quadrupled.[9]

Britain, for its part, tolerated the potential competition from New England (which traded with French sugar islands illegally) because the profits made could be spent on British imports. However, Christopher Hill argues:

> *The navigation laws worked increasingly to the disadvantage of North America as the population there increased... They had no tropical products to export, and they resented being dependent on Britain for all manufactured goods, instead of being allowed to develop their own industries...the American cloth industry was suppressed in 1719...in 1750 the erection in America of any new slitting or rolling mills, forges or steel furnaces was prohibited. Even a friend of America like Pitt stated that he would not allow a nail to be made in the colonies without permission of the British parliament.*[10]

Although there are differing opinions about the extent to which colonists resented the dependence on British manufactures, it was only a matter of time before the inbuilt contradictions in the system came to the fore.

In addition, Draper argues that Britain, although a mighty imperial power, was dependent on the colonies for a great deal: the provision of American timber for navy ships, pig iron for steel, cotton goods and so on. Trade was central to the accumulation necessary for the development of British capitalism, and America was the largest and fastest growing consumer of British goods.[11] Without the American colonies many British commentators of the time feared the ruin of the empire itself—and with colonial trade growing to a third of all British trade by 1775, up from one twelfth at the start of century, it is easy to see the basis of this fear.

The early British colonial system, as Draper well illustrates, was a mess. A ramshackle bureaucracy, no standing army to speak of in the colonies, the time it took to communicate with America—these were all factors which made the governing of the colonies a loose affair. The charters which had established most of the colonies determined the form of colonial government—usually a governor appointed from Britain and therefore answerable to the crown, a council appointed to advise the governor and an elected assembly. The majority of governorships seem to have been given mainly as rewards for retired colonels—many of whom did not go near the colony they governed from one year to the next and left the work to lieutenant governors. British penny-pinching meant that the governors depended on the assemblies, not on the British parliament, for their salaries, and sometimes their requests for money were denied by the assemblies.

Draper mistakenly describes this relationship as 'dual power'.[12] In actual fact, for a good 100 years there was never any doubt about who was really in control. There were not two competing sets of institutions vying for control of society. When a situation of dual power did arise it would be between the British government institutions on the one hand and entirely new, spontaneous forms of organisation on the other.

British government of the colonies was based primarily on the policy of 'salutary neglect'—a 'hands off' policy. Trade was more important than any money to be had from taxing the colonies, so the British turned a blind eye to smuggling (a very profitable British tradition anyway) and the abuse of customs officials. From early on, taxes and duties were studiously avoided by the colonists and remained unenforced by the British.

When the Seven Years War with France ended in 1763, Britain emerged victorious but exhausted and looking for someone to help pay off huge debts. Between 1763 and 1773 the British shifted several gears in their attitude to the colonies, imposing an unprecedented amount of punitive legislation. Although clearly much of this was intended to pay immediate British debts, as some of the primary sources cited by Draper show, the desire to keep the colonies dependent and therefore underdeveloped by milking them for every penny also played a part in the British government's calculations.

The end of the war had another impact in the colonies: it removed the threat of French invasion from the American doorstep. As Samuel Johnson had put it, 'We shall have our colonies at our feet, when they have an enemy near them'.[13] When the British took over Canada the threat was diminished.

Even today Edward Pearce deplores this move, arguing that the French 'always kept the colonists respectful' and, 'Alas, we...liberated the Americans from French surveillance'.[14] The removal of the French threat probably did put independence on the agenda earlier, but it was not a key factor. The developing commerce in New England, the expansion of slave plantations, the growth of population and trade continued while the French were there. The possibility must be considered that eventually the French would have had to be fought by the colonists, as the British were, for ultimate control in the colonies. The break from Britain would at most have been postponed, not prevented. Pearce underestimates the centrality of colonial trade to the British if he thinks 'salutary neglect' could have moved on to a mutual parting of the ways.

The growing crisis

British legislation hit the colonists from all sides: The Proclamation of 1763 prevented them from settling the area to the west of the Allegheny mountains; the Sugar Act in 1764 tried to enforce the old Molasses Act, charging merchants three pence for every gallon of imported molasses as tax, to pay for the presence of British troops, some of whom were to be stationed in Boston and New York; the Quartering Act in 1765 put the burden of housing the British soldiers, serving under General Gage, onto the colonies.

These moves were all resented, and opposed to varying degrees, but the 1765 Stamp Act provoked mass outrage, and put the question of parliament's right to impose taxes on the colonies on the agenda. The Stamp Act involved duties on court documents, church correspondence, liquor licences, land transactions, wills, passports, dice, and a host of other items.[15] In addition, taxes had to be paid in sterling, which was not easy to come by. If parliament could impose stamp tax, the colonists reasoned, it could levy a tax 'for the light of the sun, the air we breathe, and for the ground we are buried in'.[16]

The Americans, in opposing the taxes, asserted that they represented an infringement of rights that had been laid down in the original colonial charters, that parliament had no right to tax them without consent or fair representation.[17] The mass of society quickly became drawn into action. In Boston in August 1765 a movement of intellectuals, lawyers, artisans and labourers burnt an effigy of Andrew Oliver, who was to be the stamp distributor, and destroyed the building they thought was to be the stamp office. The 'lower orders' in the towns were to provide the ground troops of the revolution. Any illusion that the revolutionary period was a polite exchange of words between gentlemen should be rudely dashed by the actions of the crowds.

On 26 August, a crowd shouting 'Liberty and property' marched to the home of lieutenant governor Hutchinson and destroyed it with axes. Governor Bernard of Massachusetts complained that 'Boston is the possession of an incensed and implacable mob'.[18] The response to the violence, even from some who had encouraged it, was to condemn it. John Adams, for instance, condemned the 'blind undistinguishing rage of the rabble'.[19] Sam Adams, altogether more radical and the central revolutionary figure in Boston, qualified his disapproval: 'It was not to be wondered at, that among the common people such steps were taken as could not be justified, it being frequent in populous towns when grievances are felt'.[20]

The masses who tore down Hutchinson's house were motivated both by opposition to the Stamp Act and the deeper inequalities visible in colonial society; in New York, of 560 taxpayers, 495 held property worth less than

£10. The property of 158 was only rated at £1 while only ten owned property worth £40 or more—including the Van Rensselaer family who were between them worth £395.[21]

Before the Stamp Act, there had already been internal rebellion in some colonies—in 1771 in North Carolina the Regulator movement was formed in response to unequal taxation and marched on the governor's palace. Six rebels were hanged for treason. The revolt had been crushed by Whigs who later became American patriots. Hatred of these leaders led many former rebels to side with the British in the revolution. In fact, the greatest loyalist base was among the dispossessed in the South, rather than among Northern merchants as simplistic accounts of the revolution argue.

Farmers in Pennsylvania had marched on Philadelphia in 1763. Land rioters in New Jersey, the Hudson Valley and the Green Mountains fought against big landowners for 30 years between 1745 and 1775. In many colonies those grievances between the classes became crystallised against the British during the revolutionary crisis and fed into the campaign against the Stamp Act. Merchants in the colonies boycotted British goods. British merchants, panic stricken about their profits, cut back on credit to the South, the effect of which was to force the planters further down the revolutionary road.

In colony after colony the houses of Stamp Act supporters were wrecked. In New York 'a crowd made up of 400 to 500 seamen, 300 carpenters and many others destroyed the house of Major James, a British official, who had boasted that he would 'cram the stamps down [the people's] throats with the end of his sword'.[22]

In each colony revolutionary groups sprang up to organise the protests. Central to them everywhere were merchants and intellectuals like Sam Adams in Boston, John Lamb in New York, Christopher Gadsen in South Carolina, small merchants like Isaac Sears in New York, and artisans like Paul Revere in Boston. As the Sons of Liberty they organised a mass, popular movement against the British in the cities. In addition, 'these revolutionary bodies…consisted of artisan shopkeepers, mechanics, day labourers, carpenters, joiners, printers, shipwrights, smiths, calkers, rope-makers, seamen, masons and other members of the lower classes'.[23] These were men whose own grievances could be linked with those of the merchants against the British. As one leaflet put it:

> They will…undersell our merchants, till they monopolise the whole trade. Thus our merchants are ruined, shipbuilding ceases. They will then sell goods at any exorbitant price. Our artificers will be unemployed, and every tradesman will groan under dire oppression.[24]

The rebellion in America and pressure from British merchants and manufacturers suffering from the boycott of British goods led the British government to repeal the Stamp Act. But, determined to reassert parliament's authority in the colonies, it linked the repeal to the passing of a Declaratory Act which reasserted parliament's right to 'bind the colonies...in all cases whatsoever'.[25]

The struggle against the Stamp Act led to a questioning of British authority, but most merchants wanted compromise not independence. James Otis, a Massachusetts lawyer, who with one breath asserted that 'taxes are not to be laid on the people but by their consent in person or by deputation', answered the question of what would happen if the British would not back down through force of argument with, 'Let parliament lay what burdens they please on us, we must, it is our duty to, submit and patiently bear them till they will be pleased to relieve us'.[26]

The contradictions obvious in Otis's writing appear time and again throughout the decade before the war with Britain finally broke out: some of the leading ideologists of the revolution spent years struggling with attempts to marry obedience to the British king-in-parliament system with their increasing desire to be free of the constraints placed on them and their trade by the colonial relationship. The search for a compromise with Britain was to continue even after the war started, so tied to the imperial relationship were the leaders of the revolution. Had a middle road been available they certainly would have taken it. In addition, in Boston and New York the merchants and lawyers who had initially stoked the protests had lost control of them. Fear of the social discontent they had unleashed was an important factor in their reluctance to carry the revolution through at certain times.

In 1766 the British government's new head of the Board of Trade, Charles Townsend, attempted to renew British control over the colonies. He passed a series of acts: a Restraining Act, punishing New York for defying parliament's order two years previously to house soldiers by refusing all its legislation, and a series of import duties on glass, lead, paint, paper and tea. With the money from these taxes, Townsend planned to pay British governors and officials, freeing them from dependence on the colonial assemblies and therefore assuring Britain of their loyalties. Sam Adams tore into this policy:

> *The people's money being first taken from them without their consent, is appropriated for the maintenance of a governor at the discretion of one in the kingdom of Great Britain upon whom he absolutely depends for his support. If this be not a tyranny I am at a loss to conceive what tyranny is.*[27]

He called for immediate action to repel the latest British attack: 'Let every town assemble. Let associations and combinations be everywhere set up to consult and recover our just rights'.[28] The Sons of Liberty, led by Sam Adams, backed by wealthy merchants like John Hancock who were suffering under the duties, and with a mass base in the population of mechanics, artisans and sailors, led the charge. Boston voted to boycott all non-essential imports from the British. Connecticut and Rhode Island followed suit. The temperature rose. John Dickinson wrote, 'We are taxed without our own consent...We are therefore—SLAVES'.[29]

Yet again the mass of the population was central to defeating the acts. A Board of Commissioners was established to collect the duties. Governor Bernard refused to help them if the people of Boston attacked them and sure enough, on 10 June 1768, the ship *Liberty,* owned by John Hancock, was seized at Boston harbour, precipitating a riot in which customs officers were attacked and had to flee to the British fort, Castle William. Governor Bernard feared an insurrection and called for troops to be stationed in Boston. In New York, General Gage called for force to put down the revolt.

The merchants blamed parliament alone for the repressive legislation and urged the king to support them. Their approach shows how badly sections of colonial society still wanted compromise with Britain. Dickinson summed up the contradiction, saying, 'We are as much dependent on Great Britain as a perfectly free people can be on another'.[30] If in truth the colonists were endowed with the same freedoms as Englishmen, as they claimed, why were they dependent at all? The choice was to accept their unequal relationship with Britain or to assert their rights, which led logically—though they resisted it—away from dependence.

From 1768 to 1769 imports from Britain nearly halved; in New York they went down to a fifth. Benjamin Franklin, though 'not yet ready for political independence, was already a prophet of economic independence', according to Draper. He wrote to Philadelphia merchants that to take advantage of the lack of British goods on the market, and 'to manufacture for themselves, or use colony manufactures only' was the means 'of establishing the freedom of our country entire'.[31] Daniel Dulany also saw the potential to hurt the imperial master:

> By a vigorous application to manufactures, the consequence of oppression in the colonies to the inhabitants of Great Britain would strike home, and immediately. None would mistake it.[32]

Yet the political arguments for independence lagged behind the realisation that it was economically feasible. As Draper shows, the British saw the possibility of colonial independence before most colonists did. Lord Hillsborough made the British position crystal clear: 'The colonies have…imprudently united to dispute the right of parliament, which…we cannot permit to be called into question… It is essential to the constitution to preserve the supremacy of parliament inviolate'.[33]

That the British were willing to use force to preserve the supremacy of parliament was graphically illustrated in March 1770. In February a child had been shot and killed by a detested customs informer during a demonstration and thousands had attended the funeral. These tensions boiled over on 5 March when a crowd taunted soldiers guarding a customs house and began to throw snowballs at them. The soldiers responded to snow with bullets, killing five.

Draper's account of the massacre is not a sympathetic one. He considers the incident as blown-up out of all proportion by the revolution's propagandists:

> …*the Boston leadership decided that the 'massacre' lent itself to a campaign against a British 'standing army' in the colonies. It mattered little that the altercation had been set off by nothing more than an exchange of insults…that a colonial mob had attacked a British sentry, that no official order was given to the soldiers to fire…*[34]

This cynicism is picked up by Edward Pearce in his review. Referring to the revolutionaries' 'bombastic self pity',[35] he seems to hint that if more had been killed it might have been worth shouting about. Pearce and Draper both underplay the impact of the massacre. No blood had been spilt in the conflict with the British up to this point. The Boston massacre raised the temperature in the colonies and steeled the spines of many Bostonians against their imperial master. The event genuinely aggrieved and angered people, who were not simply the dupes of their leaders, as Pearce implies, but were becoming radicalised, rallying behind those leaders in greater numbers after the murders and beginning to organise and arm themselves.

What Draper does show is the fear and panic the revolt generated amongst the British representatives in Boston and the total lack of remorse on the part of the British for the massacre. He quotes General Gage writing frantically to London that, 'government is at an end in Boston, and in the hands of the people'.[36] The response from the British was to defend their right to exercise absolute authority over America. Lord Hillsborough set out the position:

> *When the colonies rise up in a daring opposition to all legal authority; when they deny their dependence upon this kingdom; when…they will not suffer English vessels to carry on a peaceable commerce, nor indeed any commerce at all with English ports in America; who…will assert that the mother*

*country should…tamely suffer injury after injury, and allow the colonies to
rule her with a rod of iron, for fear of being charged with a severity of
conduct towards the colonies?*[37]

Despite the bluster, the British government was forced to repeal all
but one of the Townsend Duties—that on tea—in 1770. The duty collected on tea had brought in a pittance: the British held on to it for no
other reason but to make clear to the colonies that parliament would not
renounce its right to tax them. The partial repeal of the Townsend Acts
was followed in May 1773 by the Tea Act, which bailed out the East
India Company by allowing it access to American markets. The other
side of the Tea Act was shown by North's statement that 'no doubt there
are political reasons… I know the temper of the people there is so little
deserving favour from hence…'[38]

The Tea Act was met with a storm of protest. It was described by a
meeting in Philadelphia as 'a direct tendency to render assemblies
useless, and to introduce arbitrary government and slavery'.[39] In Boston,
the campaign against the British—organised through a Committee of
Correspondence, a network of which sprang up to direct the revolt—
resolved that no one should aid the sale of tea.[40] Medical reports were
even published claiming that tea was poisonous! On 28 November 1773 a
ship with tea on board was turned away at Boston harbour. Public notices
were posted by the Sons of Liberty warning local tea agents that they
would be considered 'wretches, unworthy to live, and made the first
victims of our resentment'.[41]

Three ships made the mistake of risking a stay in the harbour. The
word was given by Sam Adams at a town meeting, the ships were
boarded by men disguised as Mohawk Indians, and 342 chests of tea,
worth £10,000, were smashed open with tomahawks and dumped over-
board in what has become known as the Boston Tea Party. Tea agents
fled Boston and from then on Boston was, in effect, lost to the British
Empire. Thomas Jefferson described the events as the dawning realisation of the colonists of their ability to force change: 'An exasperated
people, who feel that they possess power, are not easily restrained within
limits strictly regular'.[42] By the end of 1774 virtually every colony had
experienced an anti-tea protest. Drinking tea was made an offence.

To the colonists, parliament's action was pure tyranny. Throughout
1774 and 1775 colonial newspapers, mushrooming in number, attacked
British rule. Even at this stage, however, any mention of independence
was used as a threat to the British—not as a practical aim. To the British,
the refusal of the colonies to submit to parliament's taxes was treason,
and the attack on East India Company property was an outrage.
Reasoning that if they could crush the rebellion in Boston all other resistance would crumble, North passed a series of 'Intolerable Acts' in

March 1774. Boston's port was closed—effectively starving the town of income—governors could replace judges and sheriffs at will, and the British could appoint all members of the council.

Totally against British expectations, the Intolerable Acts served to unite the colonies behind Boston. All out conflict was imminent: Massachusetts now really was facing a situation of dual power—with two sets of institutions competing for the loyalty of the population. The momentum of the revolution was sweeping the compromisers aside. The radical leaders now coming to the fore—men like Sam Adams and Thomas Jefferson—were influenced by the democratic, rational and scientific ideas of the Enlightenment. They looked back to the English Revolution for inspiration, and their ideas filtered down and enthused the general population. During the war for independence, George Washington was referred to by a Massachusetts farmer as 'Great Cromwell'.

The old order was collapsing. Committees of Correspondence spread quickly—by February 1774 all the colonies but North Carolina and Pennsylvania had established committees which rivalled the British-installed governors for power. In September delegates from all colonies except Georgia held a Continental Congress in Philadelphia to decide their response to Boston's call for an end to all trade with Britain.

Reconciliation with Britain looked more and more impossible, but still some delegates clung to it, and the congress as a whole, after two months, had still made no firm statements of independence. It did, however, send a message to General Gage, now governor of Massachusetts, warning of the 'horrors of civil war' if the punitive measures against Boston were not revoked.[43] Crucially, the delegates set up a Continental Association, which met Boston's call for a boycott of British trade, and also called for internal discipline and organised committees to oversee both. The association tied together the committees in a unified organ of revolutionary struggle: 'The first steps toward destroying British power and toward creating a revolutionary government had been taken'.[44]

Once more the agreements were enforced by action from below: the first collective action to enforce non-importation was that of 41 blacksmiths of Worcester County in Massachusetts, who agreed not to work for violators or known Tories. Parliament's authority was denied in every quarter. The king's authority held, but was being questioned. Benjamin Franklin, who had left England accused of being a traitor for publishing letters from royal governors which urged force against the insurgent colonies, now 'saw more mischief than benefit from a closer union' with Britain due to the 'extreme corruption prevalent among all orders of men in this old rotten state'.[45]

Sam Adams had already moved some way down the road of colonial self rule three years earlier, when he stated that 'the people and their representatives have a right to withstand the abusive exercise of a legal and constitutional prerogative of the crown'.[46] Thomas Jefferson was far less respectful than many when, in *A Summary View of the Rights of British America* (1774), he wrote to the king of the colonists' grievances, asserting that,

> ...*kings are the servants, not the proprietors of the people. Open your breast, Sire, to liberal and expanded thought. Let not the name of George III be a blot in the page of history.*[47]

But Franklin and others were nonetheless reluctant to prosecute a war with such a 'near relation'. Franklin himself proposed a partnership between the king and colonies that by-passed parliament. However, Lord Dartmouth circulated a speech from the king urging any necessity to protect parliament's right to legislate—helping to break the illusion that the king could somehow be separated from parliament in relation to the colonies.

In Massachusetts, there was no such confusion: 'Our people...are everywhere learning the military art—exercising perpetually...', 'are formed into companies, are armed'. John Adams estimated that 15,000 men could be called on to fight.[48] Across the country rebellion swelled: in New Hampshire 400 colonists seized Fort William and Mary, taking prisoners and making off in a boat with 100 barrels of gunpowder, returning the following day for the muskets and cannons. In Boston the British were under siege: General Gage had nowhere near enough forces to deal with any serious revolt—there were only 6,000 troops in Massachusetts by 1775. His every order was defied. He could get no barracks built for his soldiers; carpenters in Boston and in New York refused to do the work. British boats were sunk and supplies prevented from reaching the army. Repeatedly he begged London for extra forces, to no avail. Gage was to admit later that the British had been unprepared to oppose so general a revolt.

Resolutions were passed in committees up and down Massachusetts denouncing British rule. In October the provincial congress set up a Committee for Defence and Safety with orders to assemble a militia as soon as considered necessary, to form companies and to seize British ammunition and weapons stores. The militias had existed in peacetime but now took on a new spirit, with new leaders. A key force, the Minutemen (so called because they were ready to act at a minute's warning) were the organised heart of the militia.

The assumption by the British that Boston would be left to fight alone was very much mistaken: the level of resistance and militancy was higher in that town than anywhere, and it provided a beacon of revolution, inspiring others across the country. The other colonies armed and trained themselves in Boston's defence as well as their own in an unprecedented show of unity.[49] In Concord, Massachusetts, on 16 April 1775, James Warren wrote to his wife:

All things wear a warlike appearance here. This town is full of cannon, ammunition, store, etc, and the army long for them and they want nothing but strength to induce an attempt on them. The people are ready and determined to defend this country inch by inch.[50]

War was three days away.

On 19 April, under orders from London, Gage sent 700 armed men to Concord to destroy the colonial arms depot. One detachment went through Lexington where they met 75 armed Minutemen. The battle that ensued left eight Americans and one British soldier dead. At Concord the British were met by 450 militiamen, organised by the Sons of Liberty, who forced the British to retreat to Lexington. By now 'the countryside was up in arms'.[51] Despite 1,000 reinforcements, the British were quickly outnumbered by militiamen who drove them back to Boston—killing 73 during the retreat. In any case, the stores had already been moved. The word had spread that the army was on its way, probably even before Paul Revere made his famous ride to sound the alarm throughout the countryside that 'the Regulars are coming'.

News of Concord spread to New York where the Liberty Boys made an assault on the arsenal, distributed arms and took over governing the city. The 'shot heard around the world' had been fired, and—after six years of war in which the colonies united against their old colonial master—America was to emerge as an independent nation.

Draper's account ends in 1775 with the outbreak of war. He sees the War for Independence as the outcome of both sides 'rubbing each other up the wrong way for about ten years' and 'spoiling for a fight'.[52] However, the colonists were not *uniformly* spoiling for a fight at all—Draper makes no mention of the very powerful pressures there were on the merchants especially, to hold back from the conflict.

The reality was that, as most of his sources illustrate, many leaders of the revolt against Britain were reluctant to endorse the separation from Britain which war would inevitably bring. Many in the alliance of planters and merchants feared for their economic survival. They resisted the British but, each for their own reasons, bemoaned the corruption of a basically good system rather than wished for an end to it altogether. They also had good reason to be afraid of the social forces that such a rupture would unleash. Their fear is illustrated by Gouvernor Morris before the war:

The mob begin to think and to reason... I see with fear and trembling, that if the disputes with the British continue, we shall be under the domination of a riotous mob. It is in the interest of all men, therefore, to seek for reunion with the parent state.[53]

Independence, when it came in July 1776, represented the last option and was not articulated even after hostilities had started: 'The war broke out even before the entire American radical side fully believed that independence was what it was fighting for'.[54]

Draper's book, which rightly sees economic factors as absolutely central to the revolution, has come under attack from another American historian, Eric Foner, who argues that Draper misses out ideological factors altogether. This is, in part, a justifiable criticism. But Foner overstates his argument, claiming that the 'coming of the revolution must be explained in large measure in ideological terms'.[55] In fact, the ideology of the revolution lagged behind economic developments: Tom Paine was the first to call for a final break with Britain, almost eight months after the war with Britain had started! The revolutionaries did not know in advance where their struggles would lead. As the French revolutionary St Just would say a few years down the line, 'The force of circumstances perhaps leads us to results we had not thought of'.[56]

Draper is right to stress that the increasing population and wealth of the American colonies was indeed driving them along the road to independence, and that ultimately the frustration caused by the immovable object that was Britain was to prove too much. He makes clear that the revolution was the result of a combination of several factors, arguing that the ideological arguments which were working their way towards independence were not sufficient to transform America's colonial role:

> ...*without the growth of population, the sense of British economic dependence on colonial trade, the expansion of far-flung colonial economic interests straining to be released from imperial restraints, the military experience gained in the Seven Years War, and the rise of a new colonial generation unburdened by attitudes of deference and obedience, it would have mattered little who was right or wrong in the ideological, constitutional, and political arguments of the years after the Stamp Act.*[57]

This is true—economic interests shaped the new generation which, in turn, shaped the ideological arguments the revolutionaries used. But what Draper misses out is that, in addition, these ideas also impacted back on people, changing their behaviour and playing a role which was not fundamental but was important in shaping the way history was made in the colonies. The primary driving force behind the ideas enshrined in the Declaration of Independence, and more overtly in the Bill of Rights, was the dominance of the new capitalist class, and its needs and interests.

The ideas of the American Revolution are inextricably linked with the real historical process of the extension of capitalism in North America, and fed into the measures adopted by Congress in the 1780s to further that development. The mistake Draper makes is in counterposing, at times, the central importance of economic pressures to other ideological factors.

The ideas and arguments worked out in the course of the pre-revolutionary period themselves coloured the action taken against the British and drove the events forward. In combating the 'ideology' school and rightly seeing economic changes and subjective historical development as laying the conditions for the split, Draper goes too far and underestimates the role of revolutionary argument and organisation in directing the struggle.

The use of language which equated taxation with slavery and the lack of representation with tyranny in pamphlets, on notices, in sermons and speeches, clearly affected the nature of the future struggles against the British and drove the revolutionary forces forward. For example, the political arguments for independence that came from Tom Paine's pamphlet, *Common Sense*, published in January 1776, were very influential. His vision of an America of freedom, an 'asylum for mankind',[58] and his proposals for democratic government including annual assemblies and more equal representation, so 'securing freedom and property to all men'[59] tapped a nerve. *Common Sense* was immensely popular, selling over 150,000 copies, indicating that it 'said what needed saying'.[60] John Adams wrote to his wife in July 1776 that 'idolatry to monarchs, and servility to aristocratical pride was never so totally eradicated from so many minds in so short a time.'[61]

At Trenton, New Jersey, during the war when the Americans were being battered, the efforts of Tom Paine to rally the demoralised troops in the first of his *American Crisis* series of essays with his heartfelt plea to fight for liberty—'Tyranny, like hell, is not easily conquered; yet we have this consolation with us, that the harder the conflict, the more glorious the triumph'[62]—cannot be dismissed, especially since the Americans went on to win that battle. It is true that the conflict with Britain was inevitable, but the path taken was not cast in stone. This or that battle won, this or that meeting voting for or against independence, altered the balance between class forces subtly and so changed the overall picture. The struggle would occur, but the outcome of the battles between radical and conservative forces in the colonies were certainly not preordained.

In leaving out most of the stirring revolutionary literature of the time, Draper's account is drier than any discussion of revolutionary change should be, but it also leads him to an overly simplistic conclusion—to see with hindsight a clear course towards inevitable revolution. The reality is more complex: the ideological and political disentanglement from Britain took longer than the development of an objective base for independence.[63]

The upper echelons in American society—the large landowners and merchants—were tied to Britain and benefited from those ties. The outcome of the revolution was to remove British power and establish a new political order, a new state, which set itself up to further the interests of capitalist development. The revolution arose 'from and contributed to the increasing predominance of the capitalist mode of production.' It was not, however, solely the inevitable result of an emergent economic power coming into conflict with an existing one: it was also the point at which the development of capitalism in certain colonies intersected with 'conscious human agency'.[64]

In missing this essential fact Draper's book, which is a mine of information in many respects, also falls down when it comes to furnishing us with any sense of the struggle *between* colonists. Draper is so convinced that the economic relationship between Britain and America provided all the motivation for the revolutionaries' behaviour that he misses out on the pressure from below and the shared need of merchants and planters to subdue the lower orders. This is the central weakness of Draper's book. His apparent rejection of the role of human agency in the revolutionary situation makes his account veer towards one of a clash of two economic systems, inexorably moving into conflict with one another, with little sense of dynamism or the struggles that took place for the hearts and minds of colonists.

Draper's only real description of the class antagonisms is at the end of the book. Asking the question, 'Who made the American Revolution?' he answers that it was the result both of an elite which 'wanted freedom from British subjection without social turmoil and transformation' and a mass support with 'no such programme' that 'generally expressed itself in destructive local violence'.[65] Draper points to a truth when he says:

> Whatever grievances the lower orders might have had, they were mainly expressed against the British rather than their own elite. This deflection...served to divide the colonists into pro- and anti-British far more than to set one social rank against another.[66]

Except that loyalism was a complex phenomenon, often driven by class resentment, especially in the South but also in New York where the position taken in the revolution by those involved in tenant uprisings depended on the political persuasion of the landlords: 'Where landlords were Tories...tenant unrest could be harnessed to the revolution by the confiscation of loyalist lands. But…where the landlords were prominent Whigs, the tenants became vigorous Tories'.[67] What is clear is that 'the complexity of the demarcations among ordinary colonials is itself a powerful confirmation of the class antagonisms at work throughout the revolutionary period'.[68]

There were serious class tensions present in the colonies before the revolutionary crisis began—the Regulators in 1771, the land riots in New York and New Jersey that dominated the latter half of the 1770s, the burning of the governor's mansion in Boston in 1750. During the revolution, most colonies experienced social upheaval and, as the crisis deepened, the radical elements came to the fore:

> *The radical committees of the coastal towns formerly controlled by the merchants began to fall into the hands of the democratic mechanic class. In New York, Boston, and Philadelphia alike, 'nobodies' and 'unimportant persons' succeeded to power.*[69]

A mark of how determined the mood for change was is shown in Pennsylvania, where Tom Paine's democratic ideal was realised for a period. In 1776 a conference was called to form a 'new government…on the authority of the people alone'.[70] Out of it emerged the most democratic constitution of the time: guaranteeing freedom of speech, freedom of religion, and increased representation so all male taxpayers resident for a year or more could vote. There was no governor, but there were annual elections for the House of Representatives and all bills were printed so people outside the immediate political process could consider them. It was viciously denounced by the moderates as 'a mobocracy of the most illiterate',[71] and there were increasing fears among the propertied that 'artisans, small traders, farmers, and men with mud on their boots had come to power.' In opposition to these lower orders, 'Men with land, men with fortunes, men with visions of development and wealth, men with far flung connections, men with memories of the surety with which their fathers had ruled, all these were developing the distaste for state level democracy'.[72]

These men quickly sought a way of quieting people's desire for direct democracy. The struggle to pass the new constitution was bitter in places, but although they often initially had to compromise due to the force of feeling from below by confiscating Tory estates and easing tax laws, the moderates managed to break the back of 'popular democracy' and consolidate bourgeois rule. In doing so the Northern states compromised with the South, allowing slavery to continue—a factor that would doom blacks to 80 more years of servitude and would eventually tear the country apart during the Civil War.

The crushing of the more radical elements of the revolution succeeded mainly because the merchants and planters were more cohesive as a class than the lower orders, who were disparate, without collective organisation and without independent leadership. The revolution had been led by those at the top of society who were now applying the brakes. It could not have been otherwise—the historical moment belonged to the bourgeoisie, not yet to the masses in American society.

The outcome of the revolution is not part of Draper's account but, I would argue, because we get little sense of class tensions earlier in the revolutionary period from his book it is harder to understand the subsequent period. The dynamic sense of revolutionary change in which different forces within American society also struggled between themselves for power is missing, weakening an otherwise strong materialist argument.

Notes

1   'The Declaration of Independence' in M D Peterson (ed), *The Portable Thomas Jefferson* (Penguin, 1979), p235.
2   A Scardino, 'Founding fathers' tidy little war', *Independent on Sunday*, 7 April 1996.
3   S E Morison, H S Commager, W E Leuchtenberg, *A Concise History of the American Republic* (Oxford University Press, 1977), p103.
4   E Pearce, 'Meddling with molasses and tinkering with tea', *Independent Weekend*, 6 April 1996.
5   C Hill, *Reformation to Industrial Revolution* (Penguin, 1967), p283.
6   T Draper, *A Struggle for Power: the American Revolution* (Little Brown, 1996), p514.
7   Ibid, p511.
8   Quoted in G Novak, *America's Revolutionary Heritage* (Pathfinder, 1976), p118.
9   T Draper, op cit, p112.
10   C Hill, op cit, p235.
11   T Draper, op cit, p127.
12   Ibid, p41.
13   Ibid, p23.
14   E Pearce, op cit.
15   E Countryman, *The American Revolution* (Penguin, 1985) p48.
16   P Foner, *From Colonial Times to the AFL* (New World, International Publishers, 1978), p33.
17   Quoted in R Middlekauff, *The Glorious Cause* (Oxford University Press, 1982), p80.
18   Quoted in T Draper, op cit, p246.
19   Quoted in ibid, p247.
20   Quoted in ibid, p248.
21   E Countryman, op cit, p26.
22   Quoted in T Draper, op cit, p253.
23   P Foner, op cit, p34.
24   Quoted in G Novak, op cit, p122.
25   S E Morison, H S Commager, W E Leuchtenberg, op cit, p70.
26   Quoted in T Draper, op cit, p227.
27   Quoted in ibid, p379.

28   Quoted in ibid, p380.
29   Quoted in ibid, p306.
30   Ibid.
31   Quoted in ibid, p327.
32   Quoted in ibid, p338.
33   Quoted in ibid, p348.
34   Ibid, p412.
35   E Pearce, op cit.
36   Quoted in T Draper, op cit, p358.
37   Quoted in ibid, p359.
38   Quoted in ibid, p391.
39   Quoted in ibid, p393.
40   Quoted in ibid, p392.
41   Quoted in ibid, p393.
42   Quoted in ibid, p512.
43   Quoted in ibid, p428.
44   E Countryman, op cit, p106.
45   Quoted in T Draper, op cit, p436.
46   Quoted in ibid, p365.
47   M D Peterson, op cit, p20.
48   Quoted in T Draper, op cit, p440.
49   Quoted in ibid, p491.
50   Quoted in ibid, p491.
51   Quoted in ibid, p497.
52   Quoted in ibid, p502.
53   Quoted in P Foner, op cit, p34.
54   Quoted in T Draper, op cit, p511.
55   E Foner, 'Seperation Anxiety' in *London Review of Books*, 18 April, 1996.
56   St Just, quoted in A Callinicos, 'Bourgeois Revolutions and Historical Materialism' in *Marxism and the Great French Revolution* (*International Socialism* 43, 1993), p113.
57   T Draper, op cit, p458.
58   T Paine, *Rights of Man, Common Sense and Other Political Writings* (Oxford University Press, 1995), p27.
59   Ibid, p33.
60   E Countryman, op cit, p111.
61   Quoted in T Draper, op cit, p509.
62   T Paine, *American Crisis* I, in op cit, p63.
63   A Callinicos, op cit, p125.
64   Ibid, p126.
65   T Draper, op cit, p516.
66   Ibid, p357.
67   S Lynd, quoted in B Kelly, 'Who rules at home?' (academic paper, Boston, November, 1991), p27.
68   Ibid.
69   Schlesinger, quoted in ibid, p23.
70   P Foner, op cit, p39.
71   Ibid.
72   E Countryman, op cit, pp200-201.

The class conflicts which shaped British history

A review of Brian Manning, **Aristocrats, Plebeians and Revolution in England 1640-1660** *(Pluto Press, 1996), £8.99, John Saville,* **The Consolidation of the Capitalist State 1800-1850** *(Pluto Press, 1994), £8.99, and John Newsinger,* **The Fenians in mid-Victorian Britain** *(Pluto Press, 1995), £8.99*

MARK O'BRIEN

The Northern Marxist Historians group has brought together some of the best historians on the British left in this welcome 'Socialist History of Britain' series. All the authors champion the cause of the oppressed against the oppressors, the cause of the working class against the capitalists. The three editions reviewed here all stress the centrality of class to our understanding of history. They each acknowledge the role of mass movements emerging at the base of society in shaping that society. Each book also illuminates the interconnectedness of Irish history and British history through the imposition of colonial rule and the struggle for national liberation.

In his book *Aristocrats, Plebians and Revolution in England 1640-1660*, Brian Manning gives a brilliant summary of the main themes of one of the most contested areas of academic historical debate—the English Civil War. The major theme in Manning's book is a defence of class as being the key historical tool in understanding the dynamic of the revolutionary process. The defence of a Marxist account of the civil war was the project begun by Christopher Hill in 1940 in *The English Revolution 1640*. The debate, however, has continued. On the one hand, it is now widely accepted that the revolution was more than a war between the ruling elites. However, the activity of the masses, the middle layers of society and of the poor, are portrayed as having been determined by the the protagonists of the ruling groups. In such accounts the masses are never seen as having been a driving force of events in themselves. The complexities of the events, we are told, defy sharply focused Marxist categories. It is Manning's achievement that he employs the category of class and a Marxist approach to both deal with the complex realities of the civil war and at the same time cut through surface detail to expose the essential social process of the revolution. The story he gives us is one of popular intervention in the war by the poor, unlikely alliances and the contest between rival visions of the future.

Manning's view is one in which popular activity is crucial at the most significant turning points in the revolution. Indeed we see the revolution beginning with rioting in Essex. In August of 1642 the Colchester Royalist, Sir John Lucas, had aroused popular resentment because of his vigorous collection of the ship money—an inequitable naval tax imposed by Charles I. Led by John Langley, a grocer, and Henry Barrington, a brewer, at least 2,000 of the 'rude sort of people' smashed their way into the Lucas house and set about its destruction after having sacked the property down to its last metal plates and woollens. In particular they seized 'much armour and many new pistols and carbines ready charged, new great saddles and other warlike furniture'.[1] The accumulated resentments of the area were even visited upon the deceased of the house of Lucas. Contemporary witnesses explained, 'The corpses were dismembered and the rioters paraded through the town with the hair of the dead in their caps'.[2]

Against the background of the depression in the cloth trade, riots involving men and women spread through Suffolk and into Hertfordshire. Such riots pepper the further course of the civil war. As to the social character of such rebellions, we are given some insight from the fragmentary evidence available that 'weavers and rural artisans seem to have predominated…with a sprinkling of husbandmen and yeomen.' But also we learn that 'this fury was not only in the rabble, but many of the better sort behaved themselves as if there had been a dissolution of all government'.[3] And here we have a clue as to the real social dynamic of the revolution. For whilst Manning stresses the role of spontaneous uprisings, the real ideological and organisational engine of the revolution was a socially and economically heterogenous grouping that Manning calls the 'middling sort'.

The vagueness of the definition of the 'middling sort' is a necessary historical function of the social reality of the time. The rise of trade and commerce had led to the emergence of a proto-capitalist commercial class, with interests different from those of the dominant Catholic landowners. The 'middling sort', then, began with the upper layers of the peasant class whose horizons were more and more fixed upon the expanding London market. Alongside these were the traders and monopolists who were now detached from the immediate production of goods and who craved control of the urban centres and trade routes. Rising through the social hierarchy there were the merchants whose world encompassed markets and power beyond the coastline of Britain and whose domestic loyalties were both ambivalent and pragmatic. Finally there were the lower reaches of the gentry whose social insulation within the old aristocracy had worn thin and whose interests had become more and more allied with those of the rising commercial class. Manning himself is appropriately tentative about his terminology:

> *The term 'middle sort', however, is vague... A bourgeoisie is in the process of formation and the appearance of the term 'middle sort' prefigures this, but without divorcing them from the general body of small property holders...*[4]

But taking class as his starting point enables Manning to fully analyse the profoundly significant class struggle which occurred. Defending the existing order were the representatives of an ancient social order—a 'semi-Catholic' aristocracy whose wealth was based on the land. This old ruling class now also had the allegiance of the richest merchants. This elite social layer owed their wealth and privilege to the charters and trade monopolies granted them by monarchical decree. The great trading houses such as the Levant and the East India Company expanded their activities around the world. They were merchant capitalists but they were not instrumental in the development of capitalism in agricultural or industrial production.[5]

Bourgeois historians have made play of the heterogeneity of the opposing social forces of the revolution. The wealthiest of the merchant capitalists did side with the Royalists. There were members of the gentry who took the parliamentary side and even led the anti-Royalist forces. But, as Manning explains, this view operates with a superficial grasp of the historical process. For what was at stake in the English Civil War was the question of whether a new social order, one that favoured the growth and expansion of commerce, enterprise and industry, would overthrow and and replace an old and decaying order that was tearing under the strain of change and which had held back the progress of culture, trade and innovation for more than a century. The fact that in the real historical process of the revolution contradictory elements appeared in both camps should not be allowed to obscure its essential character:

> *In no conflict in history do all, or even a majority, of one class line up on one side and all, or even a majority, of another class on the other... Whether or not a conflict is a class conflict depends on the extent to which it involves class issues. In the English Civil War the reality behind the social diversity of each party was revealed by differences of ethos: an aristocratic ethos domi-nated the Royalist party however many plebians it contained, and a 'middle*

sort' ethos began to drive forward the parliamentarian party, even though it contained some aristocrats, and indeed was led by them nationally. The parliamentarian party was suffused with anti-aristocratic feelings even though it was led by aristocrats, and indeed partly against their leadership.[6]

The war between the classes was also being waged at the ideological level. On the throne sat a king who many saw as having Catholic sympathies and who, at any rate, was trying to impose a strict obedience to high church principles. The banner of the civil war under which the parliamentarians marched was that of the destruction of popery and for a more egalitarian church structure. And here again the role of popular intervention was apparent. Bishops in particular became a focus of hatred and mobilisation. At one stage, in 1641, the Archbishop of York was forced to barricade himself into Westminster Abbey as parliamentarians clashed with his armed guard. On this occasion the demonstrations against the bishops went on for three days.

The strong puritan aspect of the revolution was also clear in the passions aroused by the question of where the communion table and the pulpit should be located in the churches and in the opposition to the presence of the altar rail and to the wearing of the surplice by the priest. The communion table, it was said, should be among the people, not on the high alter. The pulpit too should not be raised, separate from the congregation. The altar rail also divided the clergy from the people and the surplice was considered 'popish'. Such issues led to physical attacks on churches and church leaders, the destruction of altar rails and the smashing of stained glass windows.

In the England of the 17th century there was no fully developed secular ideology such as that which was developed in France, partly influenced by the ideas of the English Revolution, before the French Revolution of 1789. It was religion which provided the ideological vehicle for the violent contest of world views at the heart of the civil war. It was within the parliamentarian army, however, that the importance of religion, as well as the profound democratic instinct of the soldiers, is most forcefully displayed. Within Cromwell's New Model Army suspicion of officers as being Catholics, or sympathetic to Rome, led to killings and mutiny.

In this last example Manning points to an important aspect of the attitude of the soldiers. They belonged to a revolutionary army, only recently organised as such by Cromwell. These soldiers, drawn from the ranks of the smallholders and lesser yeomanry, were acutely aware of the issues involved in the revolution. When Cornet George Joyce met with the king, he was asked from where he received his commission. He waved his sword towards his troops and replied, 'Here is my commission':

*Historians have taken this, as Charles did, as a confession that his only sanc-
tion was the sword, but Joyce surely meant just what he said: he derived his
authority from the collective soldiery of the army, and exercised it by the
advice and consent of those actually present. It is the most striking of the
many examples of the egalitarian camaraderie of the agitator movement,
especially in its earlier phases.*[7]

The English Civil War ushered in a new capitalist order based on
class, albeit in a very different manner than that of the society it had
replaced. What was to develop was a system based on the exploitation of
an industrial working class, a proletariat, by a new industrial ruling class,
a bourgeoise. A new barbarism reigned as the urban centres developed,
and a new and cruel coercion was required by the ruling class. In his
book *The Consolidation of the Capitalist State 1800-1850* John Saville
charts the rise of the capitalist state in Britain, and how it responded and
moulded itself under the onslaught of working class revolt and became
adapted to the requirements of the now established capitalist class.

Saville has made a distinctive mark in history debates on the left. He
is particularly keen to emphasise the activity of all layers of society in
the historical process. It is not enough, in Saville's view, to talk only of
'history from below'. In the capitalist era the activity of the capitalist
class must also be considered to give us a complete account. The
strength of this perspective is that Saville brings out in clear relief the
capitalist nature of the state and its essential hostility to the working
class. But perhaps it places too great an emphasis on the power of the
state in defeating the working class in the middle of the 19th century. In
so doing Saville understates the subjective political weaknesses of the
working class itself in this period.

Saville begins his account of the development of the state with a discussion of the way in which the capitalist economy developed in the
decades after the civil war. The British state was linked to international
trade. In 1700 four fifths of British exports went to markets in Europe. A
century later this had fallen to only one quarter. The bulk of the rest of
British trade by this point was to markets in North America and the
Caribbean. Central to this expansion was the involvment of the state.
The great ports in London, Bristol and Liverpool had to be expanded.
Credit had to be made available for trading operations and exploration.
Insurance for the high risks of sea travel also had to be available.
Directly and indirectly the involvement of a state that was increasingly
orientated on capitalist activity was required.

This world expansion inevitably generated friction with other powers
which sought similarly to expand. This frequently resulted in war.
The capitalist state of the 17th and 18th centuries was above all a military state. Between 1688, the year of the Glorious Revolution, and the

Battle of Waterloo in 1815 Britain had been at war for 70 out of 127 years. Between 1689 and 1697, 74 percent of government expenditure was for military purposes. This figure did not drop below 60 percent throughout the 18th century. The result was that by the end of the Seven Years War in 1763 Britain was in effective control of large regions overseas and many of the most important sea trading highways.

The growing military and mercantile activities of the state in Britain put an increasingly heavy burden on the national purse. The collection of such taxes as the Land Tax, customs duties on imported goods and excise taxes on home produced commodities became a more and more rigorous excercise. The expansion of world markets for British produce provided a strong stimulus to domestic production and the development of industry. Coal and iron output expanded massively. New industries emerged, such as mechanical engineering and machine tool making, but they led to the perpetuation of much more primitive methods of production overseas. Saville explains, 'The remarkable expansion of the British cotton industry—representing the most modern factory production in the first half of the 19th century— had the paradoxical result of sustaining and extending one of the most primitive and certainly degrading forms of economic exploitation in the modern "advanced" world: the slave economy of the American South'.[8]

Along with this growth of industry went the growth of the working class both in numbers and in social density. The industrial proletariat displayed a particular energy and cohesiveness. Strikes became increasingly recurrent in the urban centres and workers began to show a greater potential in periodic waves of generalised activity which united the different trades. The repressive character of the capitalist state was turned more and more against this new social class.

Throughout the 18th and into the 19th century legislation designed to discipline labour and repress 'combination' came into force. Often such legislation was aimed at particular groups of workers such as that against the tailors in 1721, against the hatters in 1777 and against the paper makers in 1794. The Master and Servants Act of 1823 was the culmination of a series of laws which had regulated the relations of exploitation between workers and their employers entirely on the latters' terms. Between 1858 and 1875 on average 10,000 prosecutions a year took place under the act.[9]

But it was not just a restive British working class which the newly empowered bourgeoisie had to contend with. Over the Irish Sea powerful stirrings of national rebellion frequently brought upon themselves the attentions of the state. After the English Civil War the suppression of the Irish had been an integral and crucial part of the capitalist ascendancy. On one level the control of Ireland contributed to the growth of the economic base of developing capitalism. But a far deeper ideological and strategic significance underlay the need of the British bourgeoisie to oppress the Irish. Firstly the religion of the Irish was the very same Catholicism against which the parliamentarian armies had marched. More than this, Britain's main enemies and competitors on the high seas, France and Spain, were also Catholic countries. If Ireland were to fall to Britain's rivals, and its population would have readily welcomed them, Britain's trade to the West and to the all important markets in the Americas would have been cut off. The oppression of the Irish then was not some by-product of the Civil War, or an expansion for its own sake. It was an absolutely necesssary element in the triumph of capital in Britain and ensured its continued rule.

The key problem for the British ruling class in Ireland was simply that of trying to keep down a volatile and rebellious population who refused to accept their oppression without conspiracy, assassination and uprising. By the middle of the 19th century Ireland was more heavily policed than any other part of Britain or its empire. Visitors were struck by the omnipresence of the police.[10] It was not just that the police were a heavily armed body which made them an oppressive force. Orangeism, the ideology of the Protestant ascendancy in Ireland, was rife in the constabulary.

Saville brings our attention back to England with a discussion of the events of 1848. In Ireland this was a year of great unrest. In Europe it was a year of revolutions. In England 1848 was the year in which the British ruling class escaped the consequences of working class revolution by the skin of its teeth. On 10 October the third great Chartist petition was presented to parliament calling for workers to be given the vote. The lead up to the day was heralded by arming and military style drilling in the working class districts. The ruling class anticipated a revolutionary outburst by putting London under the command of the Duke of Wellington and fortifying every strategic centre lest they fall to the Chartists. The crucial weeks leading up to the day saw the melting away of any sentiments of sympathy for working class demands on the part of the more liberal sections of the establishment.[11]

But 1848 was not to be a year of revolution in Britain. The leadership of the Chartist movement stepped back from the brink and the moment passed. This failure of leadership is an element which Saville fails to emphasise in this account. The Chartist leaders did not realise the strength of their position. But the very scale of the mobilisation which occurred against the Chartists in 1848 was an indication of this strength. In France the demand for universal suffrage could be raised by sections of the middle class and small bourgeoisie because it did not represent a threat to their position in society given the much smaller size of the working class. In England, with the largest working class in the world at that time, a country in which more than half of the population lived in the urban areas, the possibility of the working class achieving the vote appeared as a much more profound threat to the establishment.

Saville is correct to point out the extraordinary lengths the ruling class went to to prevent the Chartist movement breaking through, but wrong not to convey the terror in which they were gripped. Certainly workers in every town and city in the country were prepared for serious confrontation. Stories also circulated of soldiers expressing sympathy with the Chartists. But in the minds of the leaders of Chartism, the first mass working class movement, the question of whether a mere demonstration of strength was sufficient or whether, on the other hand, an actual physical struggle was required to achieve its aims, was never resolved. The result was that the moment of decisive confrontation was lost. The failure was the result of a political crisis within the leadership of the working class. Seen in this light, it is a moment from which we can learn.

In 1848 the British ruling class learned a lesson it would never forget. For all its heterogeneity and the internal friction between Whig and Tory, industrialist and landowner, in the working class the rulers of Britain saw an enemy which united them.

In his book *Fenianism in mid-Victorian Britain,* John Newsinger identifies a tradition of rebellion against the national oppression of the Irish which is inspiring for the way in which it connects the struggles for emancipation with others on the English side of the Irish Sea. The Fenian movement was a mass, predominantly working class, movement which dominated Irish politics in the 1860s. Newsinger is careful to distinguish the Fenians from national liberation movements which came before and after. He is rightly wary of the tendency within Irish nationalist writing to portray the struggle against British rule as being one long mystical tradition running back into the mists of time. The many struggles against British rule have varied in terms of historical context, class composition and political aspirations. In Newsinger's treatment the Fenians stand out as the most politically advanced of the movements against the imperialist control of Ireland.

The great fact which dominated the century in Irish society was the famine which began in 1845 and lasted into the 1850s and which destroyed 40 percent of the potato crop. In these years the population of Ireland fell by 2.5 million. English Protestant landlordism had already impoverished Irish tenants with high rents and had forced a near national dependence on the cheapest and hardiest of crops—the potato. John Mitchell, the Irish nationalist, described what this meant for families in the poorest rural regions: '...how families, when all was eaten and no hope left, took their last look at the sun, built up their cottage doors that none might see them die nor hear their groans, and were found weeks afterwards skeletons on their own hearth; how the "law" was vindicated all this while; how the Arms Bills were diligently put in force, and many examples were made; how the starving were transported for stealing vegetables'.[12]

Famine relief was provided by the British. Around £7 million was spent—compared to £20 million paid in compensation to the slave owners of the West Indies after the emancipation of the slaves and £70 million spent on the Crimean War. But any sort of relief was denied to those owning more than a quarter of an acre of land. This forced thousands off their land to the benefit of the landlords. In the years of the famine perhaps 500,000 tenants were evicted.

It was not only the English landlords who benefited from the famine, however. In the middle of the century nationalism in Ireland was dominated by the moderate politics of Daniel O'Connell who adopted a conciliatory posture towards the British and whose base was firmly within the middle class. After the famine a new generation of 'Young Irelanders', as the new Irish Confederates became known, broke from O'Connell and looked instead to insurrection and alliance with the English working class. The Chartists in Britain rallied to the cause with demonstrations and rallies.

The founding of the Irish Republican Brotherhood, to become known as the Fenians, took place in Dublin on St Patrick's Day, 1858. The most prominent figure in the movement was James Stephens. Stephens had spent time in exile in France. There he made the transition from being an Irish nationalist to being a socialist and an internationalist. He was later to become a member of the International Working Men's Association of Marx and Engels. The IRB tried to organise along semi-clandestine lines.[13]

By 1865 the Fenians certainly had more than 50,000 members and may have had as many as 80,000 in their ranks, as well as 15,000 members in the British army. There was no doubting the scale and the seriousness of the Fenian threat to British rule. The internationalism of the leadership was crucial to their strategy. They looked to the national revolutionary movements in Europe and, especially, towards the United States.

As the American Civil War came to an end in 1865 Stephens's plans began to materialise. By the end of the year £250,000 had been raised. Some 120 American officers had joined the Fenians and preparations were under way to send boatloads of munitions to Ireland. However, the British had struck first with the suppression of a nationalist newspaper, the *Irish People*. Stephens suspected infiltration by the British and called the uprising off. The failure sprang from an insistence on secrecy and a form of organisation which placed more emphasis on conspiracy than open agitation. Stephens also attached too much importance to the role of the United States in his strategy for the liberation of Ireland. It was one thing to raise funds and material support from wherever it could be found, quite another to expect the government of a rising capitalist power to support an insurrectionist movement against the oppression of the Irish.

In 1867 there were preparations for a new rising in Ireland. Some indication of the seriousness of the plans under way is given by the fact that Stephens managed to recruit the experienced military adventurer Gustave Cluseret to become the commander of the Fenian forces:

> *After the Fenian episode he was to take part in Bakunin's abortive rising in Lyons and his career as a revolutionary soldier-of-fortune culminated with the command of the army of the Paris Commune of 1871. He brought with him into the Fenian movement two other European revolutionaries, both veterans of the American Civil War; Octave Farolia and Victor Vifquain. Together with the Irish American Civil War veterans, these men constituted an experienced military leadership that was easily a match for the British army command in Ireland.*[14]

The involvement of a figure such as Cluseret also places the Fenians clearly in the European tradition of 19th century social and nationalist revolutionary movements. In the event the rising was ignomiously defeated. The numbers brought into the field were disappointing and they were inadequately armed. The British often knew of Fenian movements in advance. Newsinger's account of the failure, however, could be developed further as there were more fundamental reasons for the failure.

One of the most remarkable aspects of the Fenians' preparations for their rising was the importance they attached to the role of the radical movement in Britain and of the British working class. Active, and successful, attempts were made to bring their struggle to workers in Britain. The workers' movement in 1866, however, was not the same as that of the Chartists of the 1840s. The mid-1860s marked the beginning of the era of Victorian reform. The dominant position of British capitalism in the world was secure. British colonies around the globe established markets for British produce at the expense of the decimated domestic industries of oppressed countries. Profits were high and workers in Britain discovered that if they pushed with their trade union strength they could not only improve the conditions of their exploitation but also win concessions at the political level.

The predominant mood of the working class of the 1860s, unlike that of the 1840s, was reformist not revolutionary. Both Stephens and Cluseret hugely overestimated the possibilities of a revolutionary alliance between the Fenians and the gradualist Reform League. Outside some individual members of the League support was not really forth-coming and and this helped erode confidence in the rising in Ireland.

Despite this the appeal to British workers remains one of the most dis-tinctive and important parts of the story of Fenianism. The Fenians were strong in Britain—strong enough, for example, to attempt to take the Chester castle by force of arms. But, more than this, they saw English workers not as their enemies but as their allies. Newsinger gives elo-quent testimony to their clarity on this question.[15] Newsinger's understanding of the natural solidarity of interest between workers on both sides of the Irish Sea puts his account of Fenianism in a different league to many other republican accounts of the period.

In this collection of three books, telling stories from quite different periods in British and Irish history, we find a common thread. The books tell of both victories and defeats for common people, yet what shines through in each is the importance of our history for the struggle today. We see lessons to be learned and mistakes that should never be repeated. Above all we see a commitment to the rediscovery of a history which has been hidden from our view. It is a history which equips us well for the battles ahead.

Notes

1   B Manning, *Aristocrats, Plebeians and Revolution in England 1640-1660* (Pluto, 1996), p45.
2   Ibid, pp45-46.
3   Ibid, p49.
4   Ibid, pp10-11.
5   Ibid, p63.
6   Ibid, p71.
7   Ibid, quoted by B Manning, op cit, p94.
8   J Saville, *The Consolidation of the Capitalist State 1800-1850* (Pluto, 1996), p12.
9   Ibid, p22.
10   Ibid, p57.
11   Ibid, p75.
12   J Newsinger, *Fenianism in mid-Victorian Britain* (Pluto, 1996), p4.
13   Ibid, p25.
14   Ibid, p51.
15   Ibid, p55.

From class war to Cold War

A review of George Lipsitz, **Rainbow At Midnight: Labor and Culture in the 1940s** *(University of Illinois Press, 1994), £12.95*

JOHN NEWSINGER

At the end of the Second World War the United States was gripped by the greatest strike wave in its history. Whereas the number of strike days a month had averaged less than 2 million in the first half of 1945, in September, after the end of the war against Japan, the figure was over 4 million, rising to over 8 million in October. When the new year of 1946 was welcomed in, there were over 2 million US workers, both men and women, out on strike. In January 1946 there were over 20 million strike days and in February 23 million. A comparison with 1937, the great year of labour revolt, demonstrates the significance of the post-war strike wave. In 1937 there were 4,740 strikes involving 1,861,000 workers for over 28 million days, by 1945 there were 4,750 strikes involving 3,470,000 workers for 38 million days, and in 1946 there were 4,985 strikes involving 4,600,000 workers for 116 million days. The US strike wave of 1945-1946 is one of the great episodes in working class history, a neglected turning point in the history of the class struggle, that played a decisive part in shaping the post-war world. George Lipsitz's recently revised and republished classic, *Rainbow At Midnight*, is a marvellous study of the causes and consequences of this great explosion and of its impact on the lives of working class people. It is a book of great depth and insight that deserves reading and re-reading.

In his introductory chapter, 'Why Write About Workers', Lipsitz complains bitterly about the way that the 'invisibility of labour in the present keeps us from comprehending its accomplishments and its errors in the past'. The working class has been effectively written out of US history and society, but he insists 'working people have been a powerful force for democratic change in the United States'. It was political mobilisation by workers in the 1930s that 'forced business and government to establish meaningful unemployment insurance, old-age pensions and home-loan assistance' and it was the upheaval of the 1940s that 'won a high-wage, high-employment economy responsible for what we have come to know as the American standard of living'. Nevertheless he points out that 'the working class has always functioned as a subordinate force in American history, a group capable of winning concessions from those in power, but never capable of mobilising itself and its allies sufficiently to set the direction for the nation's economic and political life'. What he hopes to do is 'to draw out…the implications of labour's struggles in the 1940s for what has happened since'. He believes that 'today's problems and tomorrow's possibilities can come into clearer focus if we understand the ways in which the political battles in the post-war era shaped the contours of the country's economic, cultural and political life'. Crucially, Lipsitz asks, 'what can we learn from labour?'

Lipsitz's own involvement with working class struggle began in the 1970s when he was working on an underground newspaper in St Louis and became involved with rank and file members of the Teamsters Union, who were campaigning to democratise their union. They provided him with 'a wonderful education about social class, the workplace, and the nature of movements for social change…their eventual defeat also educated me about the painful costs of social struggle'. *Rainbow At Midnight* was originally written as part of an effort 'to understand the origins of the problems facing that insurgent caucus of the Teamsters Union'.[1]

The war years

Lipsitz argues that wartime mobilisation transformed the US. Between June 1940 and September 1944 the US government paid $175 billion to some 18,000 companies in the form of military contracts. Of this huge sum, $117 billion went to just 100 companies and over $50 billion to the top ten. As he puts it, 'The nation's largest businesses clearly reaped the greatest benefits from one of the largest welfare projects in history— wartime industrial expansion.' The US economy practically doubled in size in the course of the war with, as one would expect, most of the benefits accruing 'to those who already had the greatest share of the nation's wealth'.

This economic expansion led to a shift in the balance of power within the US ruling class. The conservatives, representative of small corporations traditionally opposed to big government and bitterly anti-trade union, were being eclipsed by the corporate liberals, the representatives of the giant corporations that benefited most from government military expenditures. Whereas in 1939 firms with less than 500 workers had employed 52 percent of the manufacturing workforce, by 1944 they employed only 38 percent. At the same time those firms with more than 10,000 workers increased their share of the manufacturing workforce from 13 to 31 percent. This expanding sector, with its greater ability to pass on costs, was prepared to recognise trade unionism as a way of controlling and regulating the workforce. Indeed, the corporate liberals were prepared to ally themselves with 'responsible' trade union leaders and government in the maintenance of a militarised economy and US world hegemony. The challenge to this corporate liberal utopia came not from the conservatives but from the working class.

The dramatic expansion of the economy transformed the working class: the number of women workers increased by 140 percent and the number of black workers employed in industry increased by over 1 million. Whereas in 1942 blacks made up 3 percent of the workers employed on war work, by 1944 they were 8 percent. This transformation in the composition of a growing working class was accompanied by a dramatic increase in trade union membership from 7.2 million in 1940 to 14.5 million by the end of the war.

While the union leaders promised industrial peace for the duration of the war, with the Communist Party leading the way, in industry after industry across the country, unofficial 'wildcat' strikes became a routine means of self protection for millions of workers. While most workers supported the no-strike policy in principle, in practice they never allowed it to interfere with the defence of their interests. Many wartime strikes were condemned by employers, union officials and the government as being over trivial issues: a study of Detroit between December 1944 and January 1945 showed that out of 118 strikes only four were over wages with most taking place over disciplinary issues and management prerogatives. Lipsitz's discussion of this phenomenon is outstanding and worth quoting at some length:

> *A strike can serve as a tactic to obtain specific ends, but it can also function as a symbolic demonstration of power on the part of the workers. Accumulated grievances and resentments appear in all strikes in submerged form; they may not become negotiating points, and they may never appear in print as 'causes' of a strike, but any strike has a history hidden in past labour-management relations. And, of course, what seems trivial to management may have enormous importance for workers. During World War Two, unsettled grievances perpetuated onerous and perhaps dangerous working conditions while leaving company profits secure. Layoffs and production changes threatened to reverse*

wartime gains in employment, exploiting labour's cooperation for the benefit of
management. Eruptions of violence and displays of defiance released pent-up
hostilities over the hours and conditions of work. Walkouts over disciplinary
action expressed defiance of management prerogatives and voiced solidarity
with other workers. Strikes to win the right to smoke on the job asserted the
right to relax at work, and they denied to management the right to control per-
sonal habits. Demands for meat in cafeteria meals reflected anger over the
inequalities of sacrifice that created huge profits for business but shortages of
meat and consumer goods among workers.

Strikes that paralysed production graphically illustrated 'the importance of workers to society'. In wildcat strikes across the country,
'workers demonstrated their collective understanding of what only a few
would articulate as individuals: that the emerging corporate-liberal state
appeared particularly vulnerable to direct action and that workers had an
outstanding capacity for such action'. Neither the union leaders, the
employers or the government could afford to ignore this.[2]

While celebrating working class resistance, Lipsitz does not shy away
from confronting the widespread 'hate' strikes that were also a feature of
the war years. In many workplaces, white workers tried to resist the
hiring and promotion of black workers in what were often vicious displays of racism. Black workers fought back, refused to be intimidated
and demanded their rights. Lipsitz argues that it was this black determination to challenge the status quo, even in the face of sometimes violent
opposition from white workers, that stimulated those same white
workers to protest against inequality, exploitation and authoritarianism.
This determination provided the essential groundwork for what he calls
a 'strategy of popular power'. Black workers' success in claiming their
rights actually empowered the whole working class, black and white,
men and women, by showing that the way to win concessions and
improvements was to take on the employers. It was the refusal of black
workers to accept discrimination that broke down the age old divide and
rule tactic and prepared the way for the wildcat strikes of the war years.

'We will not go back to the old days'

With the end of the war the working class came under immediate attack.
The ending of overtime meant a substantial reduction in take home pay
and there were widespread layoffs. By the start of October 1945 there
were already 2 million unemployed. Many employers moved to put an
end to the gains the working class had made during the war. This provoked the greatest strike wave in American history. There were massive
strikes in the car, steel, rubber, meatpacking, oil refining and electrical
appliance industries. Lipsitz, however, focuses not on these great set-

piece struggles but on the less well known rash of general strikes that
were part of this working class revolt.

In Stampford, Connecticut, the town's largest employer, the Yale &
Towne lock company, withdrew recognition from the International
Association of Machinists. An official strike began on 7 November
1945, accompanied by arrests and clashes on the picket line. There was a
widespread fear in the city that Yale & Towne was spearheading an open
shop offensive, preparing the ground for an attempt to make Stampford a
non-union town. On 3 January 1946 there was a general strike in support
of the machinists:

> Workers all over Stampford reported to their jobs. But instead of going to
> work, they marched downtown to a mass rally. Many merchants closed their
> shops for the day. Others put signs in their windows announcing support for
> the strikers. Ten thousand people, accompanied by a band from the musicians
> union, paraded in front of the town hall, shouting slogans of support for Yale
> & Towne workers... Downtown Stampford's theatres, stores and streetcars
> closed down, while workers from industries in surrounding cities took the day
> off and sent contingents to the mass rally.

One prominent slogan on placards at the rally read: 'We will not go
back to the old days'.

The one day general strike did not win the dispute, but it encouraged
the strikers and was followed up with support on the picket line and
through collections and levies. Foremen going into work were assaulted,
had their cars damaged and their houses stoned, while on one occasion
the factory was sniped by an unknown gunman. At the end of March
1946 a series of mass pickets successfully closed the factory down and
another general strike was threatened. The company finally surrendered
in the first week of April, after five months, restoring union recognition
and conceding a 30 percent pay rise.

Lipsitz goes on to provide graphic accounts of the protracted transport
strike in Lancaster, Pennsylvania, that provoked a three day general
strike in February 1946; of the general strike in Rochester, New York
State, that put a stop to the city council's union busting in May 1946; of
the Pittsburgh general strike of September 1946 that forced the release of
union leader, George Mueller, from prison; and of the general strike in
Oakland, California, in December 1946.

Let us look at this last episode in more detail. A thousand shop-
workers, mainly women, were on strike at two city stores, Kahn's and
Hastings. Local Teamsters were refusing to cross their picket lines and
so on 2 December 1946 a convoy of scab lorries was brought in to
supply the strikebound stores. The union had advance warning:

[200 pickets] *blocked the entrance to Hastings store when the first truck drove up to it at 6am. Anticipating trouble, the Oakland police force despatched 250 foot patrol officers, 12 motorcycle riders and 12 squad cars to shepherd trucks through the picket lines at both stores. As word spread that city police were protecting strikebreaking truckers, demonstrators began to pour into the downtown area. Workers travelling to their jobs learned of the police action and took to the streets, stopping buses, streetcars and cabs. The Alameda County AFL* [American Federation of Labour] *Labour Council announced a general strike...but no announcement was necessary. The strike had already started in the spontaneous decisions by thousands of workers... In less than 24 hours, over 100,000 workers joined the Oakland general strike.*

The city was to all intents and purposes in the hands of the strikers. As far as the official union leaderships were concerned the situation had got seriously out of hand and they moved to put a stop to what amounted to a working class revolt. Indeed, Teamsters' leader Dave Beck condemned events in Oakland as 'more like a revolution than an industrial dispute'. After three days, under considerable pressure, the AFL Labour Council called the general strike off despite rank and file protests.[3]

The post-war strike wave, Lipsitz argues, 'presented the possibility of a significant break with the past', but in the end it failed to 'translate momentary victory into permanent gains'. Instead of mounting a successful working class challenge to the power of the American ruling class, the movement was successfully contained. The strike wave showed conclusively that a conservative open shop strategy to smash the unions, which had followed the First World War, was no longer a viable proposition. The unions were too strong and their members were too confident and determined. Instead, the unions had to be contained and their leaderships co-opted, welcomed into an unequal alliance with business and government. The union leaders had to be enlisted on the side of corporate America so that a rebellious rank and file could be brought to heel. This was the triumph of corporate liberalism.

The triumph of corporate liberalism

The containment of the post-war strike wave and of the threat it posed involved four initiatives by the US ruling class: first the Taft-Hartley Act to curb the rank and file and strengthen the union leaders; second the Marshall Plan combined with an urgent determination to restore world markets and third the red scare which aimed to eliminate the left and make possible the fourth initiative, the continuation of the militarised war economy into the post-war era. These initiatives are all obviously inter-related, and informing them all was the fear of the labour revolt of

1945-1946 and the potential threat it posed to the power of the ruling class. The unions were too strong to be broken, they had to be contained. This presupposed not just measures to curb the rank and file, strengthen the position of the union leaderships and purge the left, but also the maintenance of full employment and of a high wage economy. The alternative was the risk of unprecedented social unrest with the possibility of a political alternative to the establishment emerging. Lipsitz establishes the extent to which fear of the likely consequences of this unrest lay behind US government policies in the opening years of the Cold War; this is one of the book's great strengths.

Lipsitz's discussion of the Taft-Hartley Act of 1947 is particularly interesting. He sees this as the outcome of a struggle between conservatives and liberals over how best to deal with union strength. Even the conservative senator Robert Taft actually came round to see the need to strengthen the position of union leaders. As Taft put it, 'I think the men are more radical than their leaders in most cases.' The act was intended to increase the power and authority of the union leaders and to compel them by means of legal sanctions to restrain and discipline their members. Another important aspect of the act was that it denied legal protection to attempts to unionise foremen and supervisory workers. This was an important setback for the labour movement. Most union leaders were quite prepared to accommodate themselves to the act, however much they might condemn it in public. Indeed, they accompanied it with their own purge of the left from the unions, a purge that brought organising new workplaces to a virtual halt and killed off Operation Dixie, the attempt to organise the South. This is a neglected aspect of what was to be more generally known as McCarthyism. Lipsitz provides detailed accounts of this purge of the labour movement in the cities of Evansville and Fairmont which bring home how it reached down to the shopfloor. It was, as Lipsitz insists, one of the decisive moments for the working class.[4]

The boom years of US capitalism, the years of the permanent arms economy, saw organised workers successfully fight for a high and improving standard of living. As Lipsitz points out, military spending rose from $14 billion in 1950 to $53 billion in 1953 and thereafter fluctuated between $34 and $40 billion for the rest of the decade. This, he writes, 'helped launch an age of US supremacy in the world economy and led to one of the greatest growth periods in the history of world capitalism'. It also, he goes on, 'sowed the seeds for social and economic crises to come'.[5]

The great post-war boom made possible by the permanent arms economy provided the basis for an accommodation between unions, business and government. Organised US workers were to reap material benefits from the boom, although not without struggle, but the unorganised workers, mainly women and blacks, were left out in the cold. Nevertheless the boom saw a great increase in the size of the black working class and this made possible the challenge of the civil rights movement in the 1950s and the urban revolts of the 1960s. The union bureaucracies, however, clung desperately to their sweetheart relationship with employers and government, a relationship that was increasingly unrequited. By the time corporate liberalism was overthrown by the conservative revival of the 1980s, the unions were too bureaucratised, too weak, too corrupt and too compromised to offer effective resistance. The lessons of the great strike wave of 1945-1946 have got to be learned again.

The politics of spontaneity

The condition of the working class during the war, the post-war strike wave and its successful containment, are at the core of *Rainbow At Midnight*. Lipsitz also provides stimulating, provocative chapters on the rise of consumerism, Hollywood and the working class, and the class origins of rock and roll. These deserve a review in themselves, but we shall end here with a consideration of the book's politics. While Lipsitz provides a tremendous celebratory account of working class culture and revolt, the politics that inform his account are the politics of spontaneity. The working class offers spontaneous resistance to class oppression on a day to day basis and on occasion in great revolts like the 1945-1946 strike wave. His own account recognises the limitations of that spontaneity, but he still rejects the need for political organisation and leadership, for a revolutionary party. As far as he is concerned vanguardist parties are discredited by the performance of the US Communist Party in these years and by the grim reality of 'the Leninist states' in the former Soviet Union and Eastern Europe.

The first point is, as his own account shows, that the Communist Party was not a revolutionary party. Secondly, the various state capitalist regimes had nothing in common with Lenin or with Bolshevism. A revolutionary party would not make the revolution for and over the working class but would be the organisation of the most advanced workers both learning from and leading the class in struggle. Only such a party can prevent the spontaneous resistance of the working class being either defeated or contained. All of Lipsitz's own evidence points to this conclusion but he has allowed the terrible legacy of Stalinism to prejudice him against the need for revolutionary politics.

Since the original publication of the book in 1981, he has published the award winning *A Life In The Struggle*, the biography of Ivory Perry, a rank and file, working class civil rights activist in St Louis. In 1990 he published *Time Passages*, a study of American popular culture and collective memory since 1945. This volume flirts with postmodernism but still places class at the centre of its discussion of TV, film, music and fiction. He argues that ruminations on the past in the films of John Sayles, in television programs like *Crime Story*, in the novels of Eudora Welty and Toni Morrison, or in the music of John Cougar Mellencamp, equal or exceed the quality of historical acumen represented in most political speeches or history textbooks. They might not, he argues, hold the answer to the crisis in historical thinking but they go a long way to show where the answer might be found.

Most recently, Lipsitz has published *Dangerous Crossroads*, an often dazzling account of international popular music and its relationship to ethnicity, social conflict and globalisation. Here the discussion is compromised by an enthusiastic and uncritical embrace of postmodernism, although there is still much of interest. The discussion ranges from the Haitian band Boukman Eksperyans to Apache Indian, from the Neville Brothers to Fela Kuti, from Paul Simon to Queen Latifah. Somewhat surprisingly there is no discussion of Rock Against Racism and the Anti Nazi League. He dedicates *Dangerous Crossroads* to the members of United Auto Workers Local 879 at the Ford plant in St Paul, Minnesota. In 1994 this local pledged $300 a month from shopfloor collections to pay the wages of a union organiser in the Mexican car industry. This was part of the Cleto Nigmo Memorial Agreement in honour of the Mexican Ford worker of that name shot dead by police during protests against wage cuts in Mexico in 1990.[6] Lipsitz is still clearly committed to the working class and the likelihood is that the coming resurgence of working class struggle will see the postmodernism he has adopted consigned to the dustbin.

Notes

1   G Lipsitz, *Rainbow At Midnight* (Urbana, 1994), pp4-5. This is the revised edition of a book first published in 1981.
2   Ibid, pp88-89.
3   Ibid, pp120, 148-150.
4   Ibid, p172.
5   Ibid, p188.
6   G Lipsitz, *A Life In The Struggle* (Philadelphia, 1988); *Time Passages* (Minneapolis, 1990); *Dangerous Crossroads* (London, 1994).

State in debate

*A review of Ernest Haberkern and Arthur Lipow (eds), **Neither Capitalism nor Socialism: Theories of Bureaucratic Collectivism**, (Humanities Press, 1996) £32.50*

ALEX CALLINICOS

The American socialist Max Shachtman was probably the best known exponent of the idea that the Stalinist states represented some new form of class society fundamentally different from either socialism or capitalism. One of the founders of the Trotskyist movement in the United States, Shachtman broke with Trotsky and his orthodox followers, notably James P Cannon, over the Russian question in 1939-40. Shachtman and his supporters, who left the Socialist Workers Party (the American section of the Fourth International) to form the Workers Party (WP), argued that the USSR was not, as Trotsky claimed, a degenerated workers' state, but rather the first instance of a new, exploitative mode of production, bureaucratic collectivism.[1]

Though the 1940 split had a traumatic effect on the Trotskyist movement, particularly in the US, the theoretical differences between the two sides turn out under scrutiny to be less than meets the eye. Neither the orthodox Trotskyist degenerated workers' state theory nor its bureaucratic collectivist rival provides a satisfactory account of the dynamics of the Stalinist societies. Both can consequently justify a wide range of mutually incompatible political stances.

These facts have been obscured by the difficulty in gaining access to the main texts of the theory of bureaucratic collectivism. Shachtman's writings, for example, are available chiefly in a collection, *The Bureaucratic Revolution*, which has long been out of print, and many of the articles were in any case bowdlerised by the author in order to reflect his current political opinions as opposed to those he held when he originally wrote them.[2] It is partly to correct this situation that Ernest Haberkern and Arthur Lipow have brought together this collection of texts written in the 1930s and 1940s.

The overriding political objective of the collection, however, is to dissociate the theory of bureaucratic collectivism (which the editors accept) from Shachtman. There are at least two reasons for this. The first, that stressed mainly by Haberkern and Lipow, is that there is more than one version of the theory. The second, though unstated, is surely at least as important. It is to remove the theory's associations with Shachtman's political development after he broke with Trotsky.

At the time of the 1940 split, whatever his differences with Trotsky and Cannon, Shachtman was undoubtedly a dedicated revolutionary socialist, and he sought with great determination during the Second World War to root the WP in the American working class. But, faced after 1945 with the failure of this effort (particularly once capitalism entered the long post-war boom) and with the Cold War division of the world into rival blocs, Shachtman moved decisively to the right.[3]

In the global struggle between Western liberal capitalism and Eastern bureaucratic collectivism, Shachtman opted for the former. In his careful and scholarly political biography of Shachtman, Peter Drucker has demonstrated in great detail how this odyssey led him into more and more unqualified support for US imperialism—from opposition to disruptive strikes during the Korean War, through refusal to condemn the CIA invasion of Cuba at the Bay of Pigs in 1961, to support for American troops in Vietnam. By the time of his death in 1972 Shachtman was a Cold War social democrat.[4] Though many of Shachtman's followers broke with him over this move to the right, the question naturally arises whether or not it was a logical consequence of the theory of bureaucratic collectivism. Shachtman's opponents were quick to claim that it was.[5] Haberkern and Lipow do not, however, directly confront this question. Their chief concern is rather to establish that there had been *two* theories of bureaucratic collectivism, Shachtman's own and the rival version developed by Joseph Carter.[6]

Both theories emerged during the debate within the American SWP over the class nature of the USSR. In *The Revolution Betrayed* (1936) Trotsky argued that the Russian working class had been politically expropriated by the Stalinist bureaucracy. Nevertheless, the Soviet Union remained a workers' state because the means of production and foreign trade were in the the hands of the state. The bureaucracy were therefore in a contradictory position, pulled between their aspiration as a 'caste' to acquire private property over the means of production and their objective dependence on a statised economy. Revolutionaries, Trotsky concluded, must, while seeking the political overthrow of the *nomen-klatura* and the restoration of soviet democracy, unconditionally defend the USSR in its conflicts with the Western imperialist powers.

This analysis was immediately attacked by Carter and by James Burnham. Burnham argued that 'nationalised economy is *not* a sole and sufficient criterion or condition of a workers' state'. The working class could only dominate society by controlling the state; its political expropriation therefore implied its economic expropriation as well. Consequently, 'the Soviet Union is at the present time *neither a bourgeois state nor a workers' state'*.[7] Carter coined the term 'bureaucratic collectivism' to characterise the USSR. At this stage of the debate, in 1937-1938, Shachtman defended Trotsky's interpretation of Stalinism.[8]

It seems to have been Stalin's conclusion of a non-aggression pact with Hitler in August 1939 that prompted Shachtman to change his position and move towards Burnham and Carter. He now argued that the bureaucracy had consolidated itself as a new ruling class and was, by partitioning Poland between itself and Nazi Germany, pursuing an expansionist policy of 'Stalinist imperialism'. Trotsky's slogan of unconditional defence of the USSR consequently no longer applied; a thoroughgoing social revolution would be necessary to put Russia back on a socialist course.[9]

It should be clear that, as initially formulated at least, the main thrust of the concept of bureaucratic collectivism was negative. It served chiefly as an exposition and proposed resolution of the contradictions of the degenerated workers' state theory rather than a positive analysis of the nature of Stalinism. There were soon attempts to develop it into a broader ranging theory. Thus Burnham, breaking with Marxism altogether, rapidly came to the conclusion that Stalinism and fascism were both instances of a new 'managerial society'. It was this hierarchical and exploitative society, rather than Marx's classless communist society, that was fated to replace capitalism.[10] Burnham proceeded to move sharply to the right, becoming a vehement anti-Communist during the Cold War: I can remember him visiting Rhodesia (now Zimbabwe) in the mid-1960s to express his solidarity with the white settler regime as a bastion in the struggle against the worldwide Communist conspiracy.[11]

Shachtman, however, initially resisted such moves. While conceding the existence of an 'irrepressible tendency towards collectivism', he argued that 'there is no adequate ground for believing that this tendency will materialise in the form of a universal "bureaucratic collectivism".'[12] In the immediate aftermath of the 1940 split he sought to maintain his tendency within the Trotskyist tradition. Drucker calls Shachtman's interpretation 'an ambitious attempt to preserve the best of Trotsky's analysis and avoid its limitations'.[13] This is a rather charitable way of putting it, given the relative lack of new content of Shachtman's theory and the extent to which it drew on Trotsky's. Consider the following parallels. First, Shachtman, like Trotsky, treated private ownership of the means of production as a necessary condition of the dominance of capitalist production relations, thus ruling out the possibility that Stalinist Russia was state capitalist on *a priori* grounds.

Secondly, Shachtman, like Trotsky, discerned progressive as well as reactionary features in the Stalinist regime. He drew a distinction (ignored, he claimed, by Trotsky) between property forms and property relations. The former characterises very broad 'epochs' in the history of social production. The second determines the class character of a given society (what Marx called the mode of production). The October Revolution sounded the death knell of the private property form and marked the inauguration of 'collectivist property'. This 'fundamental difference between the Soviet state, even under Stalinism, and all other pre-collectivist states…is of epochal historical importance… Economic progress in the Soviet Union was accomplished on the basis of planning and of the new collectivist forms of property established by the proletarian revolution'.[14]

At the same time, bureaucratic property relations meant that the Stalinist *nomenklatura* had usurped the collectivist property form and instituted a new form of class exploitation. Nevertheless, the overthrow of the bureaucracy by the working class in a future social revolution would leave the form of property untouched: 'Just as it is possible to have different classes in societies resting upon the private ownership of property [sic!], so it is possible to have more than one class ruling in a society resting upon the collective ownership of property—concretely the working class and the bureaucracy'.[15]

Thirdly, the contradiction between property form and property relations encouraged Shachtman to follow Trotsky in seeing Stalinism as 'but a special, exceptional and temporary refraction' of the 'general laws of modern society…under the conditions of a backward revolutionary country in a capitalist environment'. His belief that the regime could not survive the Second World War encouraged Trotsky to resist the idea that the USSR was a new class society.[16] Shachtman continued to accept Trotsky's premiss that Stalinism was a fragile historical aberration unlikely to survive the war.[17]

Finally, while Trotsky advocated the unconditional defence of the USSR, Shachtman proposed to defend it—conditionally. This reflected the 'historical superiority' of Stalinism over capitalism.[18] Consequently, while revolutionaries should oppose an imperialist war of expansion waged by the USSR, 'should the character of the present war change from that of a struggle between imperialist camps into a struggle of the imperialists to crush the Soviet Union, the interests of the world revolution would demand the defence of the Soviet Union by the international proletariat.'[19]

Shachtman's first version of the theory of bureaucratic collectivism thus took over many of the features of Trotsky's analysis of Stalinism that made it so fragile and vulnerable to political events, at the same time adding to it the further contradiction that this 'belated', 'transitory', 'anachronism' was simultaneously 'a new, exploitative society'. Not surprisingly Shachtman's theory proved as vulnerable as Trotsky's to the outcome of the Second World War—not the fall of the bureaucratic regime in Moscow but its emergence as a world power.[20]

His position was under pressure from the start. Carter in particular pointed out its resemblance to Trotsky's and argued that a consistent bureaucratic-collectivist analysis required treating Stalinism as equally reactionary as Western capitalism.[21] When Nazi Germany invaded the USSR in June 1941, some members of the WP, following Shachtman's general analysis, proposed that the group call for a Russian victory.[22] But Shachtman himself, while still not ruling out the abstract possibility that it might in some circumstances be correct to take this position, refused to do so in this case on the absurd grounds that the Soviet Union had been reduced to a condition of 'vassalage' to the Western imperialist powers.[23]

Such a claim could not survive the Second World War, and in particular the Stalinist regime's expansion into Eastern Europe. Events such as the Stalinist seizure of power in Czechoslovakia signified for the Shachtmanites, in Hal Draper's words, 'the emergence of the bureaucratic-collectivist empire as a bidder for the historic role of successor to a doomed capitalism'. Consequently, 'working class revolutionists...face two enemies: a capitalism which is anti-Stalinist and a Stalinism which is anti-capitalist'.[24]

These developments made Shachtman's initial theory untenable. The 1940s saw what Drucker calls 'his step-by-step abandonment of his own theory of bureaucratic collectivism in favour of Carter's, until, by about 1948, his differences with Carter had disappeared'.[25] Shachtman, however, offered no new analysis of the dynamics of the Stalinist economy. As Tony Cliff bitingly observed, the 'only two constant elements in the theory have been: first, the conclusion that in any concrete conditions, Stalinist Russia must not be defended...; and, second, that the name of the Stalinist regime is Bureaucratic Collectivism'.[26]

Haberkern and Lipow clearly regard Carter's theory as superior to Shachtman's, and indeed take Shachtman to task for, they claim, effectively dropping it after 1948.[27] But in what sense is Carter's version of the idea of bureaucratic collectivism to be preferred to Shachtman's as an interpretation of Stalinism? Undoubtedly it is more consistent, since it does away with the confused distinction between collectivist property forms and bureaucratic property relations. But does it offer the basis of a theory of bureaucratic collectivism as a distinct mode of production? Here is a summary version of Carter's analysis of Stalinism:

Stalinist Russia is thus a reactionary state based upon a new system of economic exploitation, bureaucratic collectivism. The ruling class is the bureaucracy which through its control of the state collectively owns, controls and administers the means of production and exchange. The basic motive force of the economy is the extraction of more and more surplus labour from the toilers so as to increase the revenue, power, and position of the bureaucracy. The economy is organised and directed through state totalitarian planning and political terrorism. The toilers are compelled by the state (as well as economic necessity) to labour in the factories and fields. Forced labour is an inherent feature of present-day Russian productive relations.[28]

But this interpretation of Stalinism is as vulnerable as Shachtman's to Cliff's classic critique of the theory of bureaucratic collectivism. First, it gives no explanation of the driving forces of bureaucratic collectivism. For Carter, as for Trotsky and Shachtman, the motive for production under Stalinism is the consumption of the bureaucracy—a factor which is incapable of accounting for the immense expansion of the productive forces in the Soviet Union between the 1920s and the 1960s. Secondly, Carter grossly exaggerates the role of forced labour even at the height of the Stalinist terror in the 1930s. Thirdly, Carter, like Shachtman, provides only an indeterminate basis on which to decide whether bureaucratic collectivism is more or less progressive than capitalism.[29]

The last point is the most important one politically. It is true that Carter explicitly treats the Second World War as an inter-imperialist war in which revolutionaries should welcome the victory of neither side. But it is not clear that this correct conclusion actually follows from Carter's theory. An economy that relies chiefly on forced labour, as both Carter and Shachtman argued Stalinism did, is less progressive than a capitalist economy based primarily on wage labour, above all because it cannot develop the productive forces as effectively as capitalism can. And indeed Carter seeks to show that Stalinism cannot develop the productive forces in the way that 'early bourgeois society' did.[30] Similarly, Robert Brenner, the most sophisticated contemporary exponent of the theory of bureaucratic collectivism, argues that the Stalinist states were, in effect, like pre-capitalist societies in that they were unable intensively to develop the productive forces through technical innovations that raised the productivity of labour.[31]

It follows from such an analysis that Stalinism represented a more backward mode of production than Western capitalism. In any conflict between the two it would then surely be the duty of revolutionaries to support the more progressive side. Shachtman was thus being perfectly consistent when he wrote in 1962, after citing the classical Marxian prediction 'socialism or barbarism': 'Stalinism is that new barbarism'.[32] Haberkern and Lipow fail to appreciate the logic of Carter's theory. They ascribe to him the view that bureaucratic collectivism represented 'a step backwards for modern civilisation', but then go on to take Shachtman to task for siding with 'American imperialism as the lesser evil' in the Cold War.[33] But if Stalinism really was 'a step backwards', wasn't US capitalism, as the most powerful version of 'modern civilisation', really the 'lesser evil'?

Such confusion is, in fact, typical of this sloppily edited collection, notably in Haberkern's and Lipow's introduction.[34] Here they confront the fact that recently bureaucratic collectivism would seem to have suffered something of a setback, what with the East European revolutions and the collapse of the Soviet Union. Or has it? Haberkern's and Lipow's analysis of these world historic events is, to say the least, hard to follow.

On the one hand they say, 'What has been revealed in the past ten years, even before the fall of Gorbachev and the Berlin Wall, is that totalitarian state planning is economically regressive as compared to capitalism'.[35] Is this timelessly true? If it is, how was Stalinism able to industrialise the USSR in the 1930s? And why were the *nomenklatura* able to give Western capitalism a good run for its money over 40 years of Cold War? Or was it just sheer historical accident that the Stalinist system collapsed in the late 1980s rather than, say, in the mid-1950s?

On the other hand, Haberkern and Lipow claim that, far from the free market triumphing, a 'new system of economic exploitation in which the lines between corporate and state planning are becoming blurred' is taking shape—'this "bureaucratic collectivisation" of the capitalist system' is occurring not only nationally, but globally, in the shape of institutions such as the IMF: 'The admirable goal of international economic co-operation has been subordinated to this bureaucratisation of capitalism in the form of corporations which are themselves large bureaucratic entities not accountable to anyone except those who effectively control them'.[36]

Haberkern and Lipow are right to stress that the 1990s are not seeing the triumph of laissez-faire. The world market is increasingly dominated by giant bureaucratically organised corporations. But how does this relate to the theory of bureaucratic collectivism? Carter and his co-thinkers argued, correctly, that the Stalinist economy was a 'nationally limited economy...a huge national trust'.[37] One does not have naively to believe in fashionable notions of globalisation to see that the crisis of the Stalinist states was crucially a consequence of the inability of their nationally organised economies to compete in an increasingly globally integrated system.[38] Bureaucratic and unaccountable though current forms of capitalist organisation may be, their international extension represents a significant difference from the era of nationally organised capitalism characteristic of the first half of the century. Hand waving and incantations of the word 'bureaucratisation' are no substitute for a serious analysis of these changes.

But perhaps the most important conclusion that emerges from this

collection is the similarity between the theory of bureaucratic collectivism and the orthodox-Trotskyist degenerated workers' state theory.
This comparison is to neither's advantage. Neither gives any clear
account of the dynamics—what Marx would call the laws of motion—of
Stalinism as a social system. It is this lack of content which allows both
bureaucratic collectivists and orthodox Trotskyists to oscillate wildly
across the political scene.

We have seen how Burnham and Shachtman degenerated into what
they themselves had described when they were still revolutionaries as
'Stalinophobia, or vulgar anti-Stalinism'.[39] But Trotsky, at his last
meeting with the leadership of the American SWP in June 1940, accused
them of adapting to the 'progressive' pro-Roosevelt wing of the trade
union bureaucracy by allying with them against the Communist Party,
and failing to understand that 'the Stalinists are a legitimate part of the
workers' movement'.[40] Adherence to the degenerated workers' state
theory did not prevent ultra-loyal orthodox Trotskyists such as Jim
Cannon and Farrell Dobbs from falling into Stalinophobia.

Similarly, during the Portuguese Revolution of 1974-1975, the
American SWP lined up in effect with NATO and the Second
International by supporting the Socialist Party in its reactionary campaign against the workers and soldiers of Lisbon. The SWP justified this
position on the grounds that the Armed Forces Movement (MFA) which
overthrew the old dictatorship was seeking change by bureaucratic
methods. Meanwhile, the main Shachtmanite organisation in the US, the
International Socialists, was uncritically backing that section of the
Portuguese far left which was tailing the radical wing of the MFA and its
dreams of some sort of revolution imposed from above by the army.[41]

A theory which lacks any concrete content can be made compatible
with any political conclusions. This may help to explain why bureaucratic collectivists and orthodox Trotskyists in the United States can
today happily co-exist within the multi-tendency organisation Solidarity,
despite their apparently divergent interpretations of Stalinism.

The concept of bureaucratic collectivism is little more than a label,
defined chiefly by the negations in this collection's title—'*neither* capitalism *nor* socialism'. As to what bureaucratic collectivism actually is,
we are left none the wiser at the end of the book than at the beginning.
Its most serious and systematic interpretation, first formulated by Carter
and taken up later by Shachtman, leads to reactionary political conclusions. Haberkern and Lipow resist these conclusions, but offer instead
little but muddle. Far from, as they presumably hoped, producing an
advertisement for the theory of bureaucratic collectivism, they have
unintentionally provided a strong case for its final internment.

Notes

1   The main published sources for this controversy are M Shachtman, *The Bureaucratic Revolution* (New York, 1962), L Trotsky, *In Defence of Marxism* (New York, 1973), and J P Cannon, *The Struggle for a Proletarian Party* (New York, 1972). Invaluable historical background is provided by A Wald, *The New York Intellectuals* (New York, 1987), ch 6. For the theoretical context of the controversy and a brief critical assessment of Shachtmanism, see A Callinicos, *Trotskyism* (Milton Keynes, 1990), esp ch 4.

2   See, for example, E E Haberkern and A Lipow, *The Myth of Max Shachtman*, Appendix B to Haberkern and Lipow (eds), *Neither Capitalism nor Socialism* (Atlantic Highlands, 1996).

3   M Shachtman, *Bureaucratic Revolution*, pp305-306. For a critique of this position, see D Hallas, 'The Stalinist Parties', in *The Fourth International, Stalinism and the Origins of the International Socialists* (London, 1971).

4   P Drucker, *Max Shachtman and His Left* (New Jersey, 1994), Part II.

5   See, for example, J Hanson and G Novack, Introduction to L Trotsky, *In Defence of Marxism*, op cit..

6   E E Haberkern and A Lipow, op cit, p185.

7   J Burnham (1937) 'From Formula to Reality', in E E Haberkern and A Lipow (eds), *Neither Capitalism nor Socialism*, pp13, 15.

8   P Drucker, op cit, pp90-91.

9   M Shachtman, (1940) 'Is Russia a Workers State?', in E E Haberkern and A Lipow (eds), *Neither Capitalism nor Socialism*. See also Drucker, op cit, ch 4.

10   J Burnham (1941) 'The Theory of the Managerial Revolution', in E E Haberkern and A Lipow (eds), *Neither Capitalism nor Socialism*.

11   Dwight MacDonald took a somewhat more nuanced and less reactionary version of this position, arguing, 'Bureaucratic collectivism may or may not develop into a new form of class rule as stable as was that of the bourgeoisie', but that 'the alternative Socialist solution is still possible'. D MacDonald, 'The Future of Democratic Values', *Horizon*, VIII: 47 (1943), p318.

12   M Shachtman, 'Is Russia a Workers' State?', op cit, p77.

13   P Drucker, op cit, p132.

14   Ibid, pp80-81. It is important not to confuse Shachtman's concept of form of property with the distinction that Marx draws between legal property forms and the relations of production (understood as relations of effective control over the productive forces), particularly since some arguments against the orthodox Trotskyist conception of a workers' state can be made using either concept. On Marx's distinction see T Cliff, *State Capitalism in Russia* (London, 1988), pp184-187, 314-316, and G A Cohen, *Karl Marx's Theory of History* (Oxford, 1978), chs III and IX.

15   Ibid, p77.

16   L Trotsky, *In Defence of Marxism*, op cit, pp7, 14.

17   M Shachtman (1941) 'The Russian Question', in E E Haberkern and A Lipow (eds), *Neither Capitalism nor Socialism*, op cit, p118.

18   Ibid, p119.

19   See M Shachtman, 'Is Russia a Workers State?', op cit, p86. The passage referred to is omitted from the version of this essay reprinted in *The Bureaucratic Revolution*.

20   See, on the post-war crisis of orthodox Trotskyism, A Callinicos, *Trotskyism*, op cit, ch 2.

21   J Carter (1941) 'Bureaucratic Collectivism', in E E Haberkern and A Lipow (eds), *Neither Capitalism nor Socialism*, op cit, pp107-113.

22   E Erber (1941) 'The Basis for Defensism in Russia', in E E Haberkern and A
      Lipow (eds), *Neither Capitalism nor Socialism*, op cit.
23   See T Cliff, 'The Theory of Bureaucratic Collectivism—A Critique', Appendix 2
      to *State Capitalism in Russia*, op cit, pp336-337.
24   H Draper (1948) 'The Triangle of Forces', in E E Haberkern and A Lipow (eds),
      Neither Capitalism nor Socialism, op cit, pp136-137.
25   P Drucker, *Shachtman*, op cit, p138.
26   T Cliff, op cit, p337.
27   E E Haberkern and A Lipow, 'Myth', op cit, pp186-187.
28   J Carter, 'Bureaucratic Collectivism', op cit, p104.
29   See T Cliff, 'The Theory of Bureaucratic Collectivism', op cit. This document was
      originally written in 1948 as part of the debate on the Russian question within the
      Fourth International. Scandalously Haberkern and Lipow ignore it, along with
      Cliff's *State Capitalism*, which also began life as an FI internal document.
30   J Carter, *Bureaucratic Collectivism*, op cit, p106. On the relation between wage
      labour and the development of the productive forces under capitalism, see A
      Callinicos, 'Wage-Labour and State Capitalism', *International Socialism* 12
      (1981).
31   R Brenner, 'The Soviet Union and Eastern Europe', *Against the Current* (N.S.) 30
      and 31 (1991). See my critique of Brenner's analysis in *Theories and Narratives*
      (Cambridge, 1995), pp134-139.
32   M Shachtman, *Bureaucratic Revolution*, op cit, p32. See, for a definitive
      discussion of whether the Stalinist regime represented progress or barbarism, T
      Cliff, *State Capitalism*, pp196-200.
33   E E Haberkern and A Lipow, 'Myth', op cit, pp185, 186.
34   Some examples of Haberkern's and Lipow's poor editing: their rambling
      introduction fails to provide the reader with any proper account of the historical
      context in which the texts they collect were composed; essential background
      information about the various political tendencies referred to is also not given;
      sometimes the original publication details of texts are given, sometimes not; the
      editorial notes are frequently partisan interpolations; the editors sometimes
      become a singular 'I'. Considerations of space prevent me from considering more
      substantive muddles, for example, Haberkern's and Lipow's suggestion, following
      a hint of Shachtman's, that reformist governments may represent 'a
      "parliamentary road" to bureaucratic collectivism': see Editorial Note to M
      Shachtman, (1951) 'Aspects of the Labour Government', in E E Haberkern and A
      Lipow (eds), *Neither Capitalism nor Socialism*, op cit, p168.
35   E E Haberkern and A Lipow, Introduction, *Neither Capitalism nor Socialism*, op
      cit, pxi.
36   Ibid, ppxiv-xv.
37   J Carter, *Bureaucratic Collectivism*, p105. See also H Draper, (1948) 'The
      Economic Drive behind Tito', in E E Haberkern and A Lipow (eds), *Neither
      Capitalism nor Socialism*, op cit.
38   See C Harman, 'The Storm Breaks', *International Socialism* 46 (1990), and A
      Callinicos, *The Revenge of History* (Cambridge, 1991), ch 2.
39   J Burnham and M Shachtman, 'Intellectuals in Retreat', *New International*, V:1
      (1939), p20.
40   'Discussions with Trotsky', in *Writings of Leon Trotsky (1939-40)* (New York,
      1973), quotation from p282.
41   See C Harman, *The Fire Last Time* (London, 1988), ch 13, and, for the extensive
      debate the American SWP's stance provoked in the Fourth International,
      Intercontinental Press, 1975-1976.

Review article: coming to terms with barbarism in Rwanda and Burundi

A review of Gérard Prunier, **The Rwanda Crisis: History of a Genocide** *(London, 1995) £12.50; African Rights,* **Rwanda: Death, Despair and Defiance** *(London, 1995) £14.99; African Rights,* **Rwanda, Not So Innocent (When Women Become Killers)** *(London, 1995) £6.95; Réne Lemarchand,* **Burundi: Ethnic Conflict and Genocide** *(Cambridge University Press, 1996) £12.95; Filip Reyntjens,* **Burundi: Breaking the Cycle of Violence** *(Minority Rights Group, 1995) £4.95; Fergal Keane,* **Season of Blood, a Rwandan Journey** *(Penguin, 1996) £6.99*

CHARLIE KIMBER

Rwanda and Burundi have become synonymous with the horror of communal violence. In Rwanda, from 6 April 1994,

> *in one hundred days up to one million people were hacked, shot, strangled, clubbed and burned to death. Remember, carve this into your consciousness: one million.*[1]

As for its neighbour Burundi, 'Nowhere else in Africa has so much violence killed so many people on so many occasions in so small a space as in Burundi in the years following independence.'[2]

The suffering continues in both countries today. Tucked away in the international pages of the broadsheet newspapers are regular reports of massacres which would have been front page news if they had occurred in ex-Yugoslavia. In addition to the killings, millions of people have been driven from their homes. Many remain in fetid refugee camps and recently groups which fled from Rwanda and Burundi have continued their wars in the countries to which they have been exiled.[3]

Such tragedies pose a challenge to any theory that seeks to analyse the world rather than simply despair about its inhumanity. Why did these tiny countries, with populations of around 6 million each, become the site of such savagery? In this article I shall try to explain what has happened and, crucially, show how its repetition can be avoided. One of the most chilling aspects of the present situation is that almost all commentators anticipate further horrors in the near future in Rwanda, Burundi and perhaps Zaire as well. They are probably right, and if they are the conflict could engulf 20 million people.

Hutu, Tutsi, Twa

In both Rwanda and Burundi there is a group called Tutsis who make up about 15 percent of the population, one called Hutus which covers around 85 percent and a tiny number called Twas. It is not possible to say with certainty what happened thousands of years ago which laid the basis for Hutu, Tutsi and Twa groups. But what can be utterly disproved is the notion popularised by some newspapers and writers that bitter divisions between Hutus and Tutsis have always existed.

Most historians[4] argue that the original inhabitants of the area we now know as Rwanda and Burundi were hunter-gatherers whose modern day descendants are the tiny minority of Twa people ('the pygmies'). Later, cultivators ('Hutus') and cattle herders ('Tutsis') arrived. The authors of the African Rights book argue that:

> What appears to have happened is that about twenty generations ago, one Tutsi clan, the Nyiginya, achieved political dominance in central Rwanda. Over several centuries the Nyiginya formed the core of a state. But the political institutions that followed were a fusion of Hutu and Tutsi. In large part, before the nineteenth century, Twa, Hutu and Tutsi roughly corresponded to occupational categories within a single differentiated group. Cattle-herders, soldiers and administrators were mostly Tutsi, farmers were Hutu and the Twa were hunter-gatherers and potters.[5]

Whether you were a Hutu or a Tutsi depended largely on your lineage (what group your parents were). But as the terms also referred to social function, there was mobility: 'Individuals could and did move between the categories Hutu and Tutsi as their fortunes rose and fell, and intermarriage was not uncommon'.[6] If your father was a Hutu, you would be a Hutu. But if you then made sufficient wealth, and could buy cattle, then you might become a Tutsi. There was a ceremony of 'becoming Tutsi' which recognised this. Your children would then be Tutsi. This means that the Hutu-Tutsi distinction in pre-colonial Rwanda and Burundi was not a simple class distinction (because you could be a poor Tutsi or a rich Hutu) nor was it an ethnic distinction because you could be born into one group and die as another. Cattle were the dominant form of disposable wealth. Cattle herders were, by definition, Tutsi. Therefore society was largely dominated by Tutsis, although not all Tutsis were part of the dominant class. Moreover, all institutions and social activities displayed the mixing between Hutus and Tutsis. Everyone, Hutu, Twa or Tutsi, spoke the same language.

Power in society was extremely complicated. The king in Rwanda was a Tutsi and was surrounded by (mostly) Tutsi nobles. But the king's power did not extend evenly over the whole surface of 'Rwanda'. As Gérald Prunier demonstrates, there were 'several Hutu principalities which remained defiant until the 19th century and in some cases were incorporated only after the arrival of Europeans and with their help'.[7] Within Rwanda each locality was ruled by three chiefs, responsible for land, grazing rights and men. Often the land chief was a Hutu while the other two were Tutsis.

War with neighbouring states, which was quite common, took two forms. Often it was a largely symbolic act when armies would gather but the fighting was confined to 'champions' from either side. This sort of war was dominated by the Tutsis and the Twas. But when more serious combat was necessary, the Hutus took the leading part. For example, 'the great Rwandese conqueror Kigeri IV Rwabugiri (1853-1895), who meant business when he went into battle, preferred to recruit mostly Hutu armies who were perhaps less elegant but more efficient'.[8] So war acted as a 'social coagulant', breaking down differences. Religion was another 'shared' factor. The kubandwa cult included members of all three categories of society, although it was Hutu in origin (probably) and was (sometimes) regarded as inferior by the Tutsis.

As for the oppressed class, the peasants and landless cultivators, they were mostly Hutus but also contained many Tutsis who had slipped down the scale. They did not normally cease to be Tutsi, but they were as poor as their neighbours. So, as Gérard Prunier writes about present day Rwanda, 'Tutsi and Hutu, the notorious rival twins of Rwandese society, live side by side on the same hilly slopes—for better or for worse, for intermarriage or for massacre'.[9]

In Burundi, before the colonialists came, the situation was even more mixed because of an intermediate class between the king and the population.[10] Moreover, there were groups within the Tutsis 'known colloquially as the 'high Tutsis' and the 'low Tutsis'—and poor Tutsis often found themselves subservient to wealthy Hutus'.[11] Among the peasantry, 'relations between ordinary Tutsi and Hutu were on an equal footing and intermarriage was common'.[12] So although there clearly were social divisions between Tutsis and Hutus they were not absolute or the sole defining feature of people's lives.

What about the physical differences which so many writers mention?

[These] *have been greatly exaggerated both by European colonialists and missionaries, and later by some Rwandese politicians and the Western media... Rwandese tell an individual's group by his or her lineage, not by his height or straightness of nose.*[13]

Any differences which did exist would in any case be blurred by intermarriage; in Ntarama in the southern lowlands of Rwanda a third of Tutsi daughters were married to Hutus.[14]

Any belief in defining physical differences between Tutsis and Hutus should be shattered by one remaining fact: victims of the slaughter of 1994 were selected on the basis of their identity cards. Many Tutsis survived by having a forged Hutu card. The second most common way of choosing victims was to ask people the background of others in their village. In other words it depended on one person revealing another to be a Tutsi.[15] There is another powerful example: the leader of the Hutu militias, the *interahamwe*, in 1994 was Robert Kajuga, a Tutsi whose father had opted for a Hutu identity card.

The Europeans in Rwanda and Burundi

Whatever the complexities of early Rwanda and Burundi, these societies were fundamentally altered with the arrival of colonial powers. As part of the 'scramble for Africa' between rival European states, Rwanda and Burundi were seized by Germany. The colonisation began around 1890 and developed over the next decade. In the late 1890s Rwanda and Burundi, which had been separate states for centuries, were merged into a single colony as part of German East Africa. The German colonial presence was very limited,[16] but began to transform the relation between Tutsis and Hutus. 'When due to lack of manpower the Germans could not directly control a certain area...they were not above sub-contracting local control to Tutsi chiefs, who, secure in the white man's support, acted as rapacious quasi-warlords'.[17]

This transformation was much accelerated when the Belgians occupied German East Africa in 1916. At the end of the war they separated Rwanda and Burundi once more and began to construct a system that would guarantee stability for the coffee and ivory trade. It was some time before the Belgians instituted a fully fledged system of colonial rule, and their strategy was to administer the country directly through Africans.

In Rwanda there was at first some attempt to understand the existing structures so that they could be absorbed into Belgian control.[18] But the Belgian ruling class, who (like the British, the French and others) acted in the most brutal fashion towards colonised Africans, were not willing to spend the time and energy dealing with the 'intertwined fingers' of Rwandese Tutsi-Hutu relations. It was much easier to divide society between Tutsis and Hutus and ally with one group against the rest.[19]

The ruling class, which had formerly been dominated by Tutsis but still contained elements of Hutu and Twa, was changed into one almost wholly made up of Tutsis who were willing to act entirely in accordance with the colonialists' wishes. Gérard Prunier quotes from a Belgian colonial report to show how such changes were justified; the Twas were 'small, chunky, muscular and very hairy: he is quite similar to the apes whom he chases in the forest'. The Hutus 'are generally short and thickset with a big head, a jovial expression, a wide nose and enormous lips'.[20] But the Tutsis were definitely superior beings:

> *The Tutsi of good race has nothing of the negro, apart from his colour. He is usually very tall, he is usually very thin. His features are very fine. He is a natural-born leader, capable of extreme self-control and of calculated good-will.*[21]

Given the racist assumptions about central Africa, most outsiders decided the Tutsis had come from a long way away. The famous British explorer of the Nile, John Hanning Speke, decided without a shred of evidence that the Tutsis had come from southern Ethiopia. The Belgian administrator Count Renaud de Briey 'coolly speculated that the Tutsi could very well be the last survivors of the lost continent of Atlantis'.[22]

The Belgians rammed through a series of measures which utterly transformed the social structure. Christianity became the state religion and the church controlled education. The elite Tutsis flocked to become Catholics as a badge of their new identification and to get a chance of decent schooling. The previous system of having three chiefs for each area, one at least of whom was normally a Hutu, was replaced by having a single chief for every locality. By the end of the Belgian presence in 1959, 43 out 45 Rwandan chiefs were Tutsi as well as 549 sub-chiefs out of 559.[23]

This control of the state meant the Tutsi elite could grab economic wealth. Common grazing areas and collectively held land could be taken by the state after 'due compensation'. With the backing of the Belgians, the Tutsi elite grabbed much and paid out little. At the same time the Belgians were demanding huge amounts of forced labour from the peasantry. Various compulsory work activities for the state could absorb over half of a man's time. Those who refused such work were abused and attacked. A UN delegation to Rwanda in 1948 found that, of 250 peasants they interviewed, 247 had been beaten up, usually many times.[24]

The European presence 'froze' the movement between groups by instituting identity cards and increased the class identification by favouring the Tutsis for powerful positions and access to wealth. The majority of Tutsis however, remained poor. A survey in the mid-1950s of a representative section of the population excluding holders of political office showed:[25]

Group	No of families	Average income (Belg. Fr.)
Tutsi	287	4,439
Hutu	914	4,249
Twa	2	1,446

Thus there is almost no difference between Hutus and Tutsis. However, as Gérard Prunier writes:

> The racialisation of consciousness affected everybody, and even the 'small Tutsi', who did not benefit from the system in any way, started to believe they were indeed a superior race and that under the same rags as their Hutu neighbours wore, a finer heart was beating. The Hutu, deprived of all political power and exploited by both the whites and the Tutsi, began to hate all Tutsi, even those who were just as poor as they.[26]

Prunier points to a process whereby colonialism laid the basis for horror. 'Although Rwanda was definitely not a land of peace and bucolic harmony before the arrival of the Europeans, there is no trace in its pre-colonial history of systematic violence between Tutsi and Hutu'.[27] Afterwards such conflict was common and murderous.

A similar but less clear cut process occurred in Burundi. The Belgians again employed divide and rule, but the existence of a separate princely caste meant the division between Hutu and Tutsi was not the sole or defining element in society. Instead it meant that the Belgian rulers both gave privileges to the Tutsi elite and also worked alongside a group which was hostile to both Hutus and Tutsis. The result was a series of anti-colonial revolts—Rubengebenge (1912-22), Inamuvyeyi Nvavyinshi (1922), Runyota (1922) and Inamujandi (1934). These were not the revolt of one ethnic group against another but (mainly) the revolt of subject peoples against the Europeans.

These Burundi revolts often had ethnic elements (for example some explicitly raised the question of the rich Tutsis selling out to the Belgians, but then went on to target all Tutsis), but they were not simply ethnic. Unlike in Rwanda, it was not the period of colonial rule itself which sealed the ethnic division, it was the manoeuvres that accompanied its end.

Independence and new rulers—Rwanda

As the rest of Africa began to achieve independence, the Tutsi elite in

Rwanda became supporters of swift removal of Belgian control. This seemed a strange reversal for a group who had prospered mightily from colonialism. But they believed that the longer independence was delayed, the more likely it was that the Hutus would demand majority rule.

The shift meant the Belgian colonialists began to see their Tutsi allies as dangerous and communist-inspired supporters of national freedom. Of course the Tutsi elite were nothing of the sort. They were not at all interested in transforming the conditions for the vast majority, Tutsi or Hutu, but they were determined to hang on to their privileges in a new world and the only way they could see to do it was to take the radical step of rapidly bundling the Belgians out.

Equally remarkably, the tiny numbers of the Hutu elite, whose group had suffered most from Belgian colonialism, were less keen on quick independence. Instead they stressed ethnicity and a big role for the Belgians in policing the transition. The first manifesto of PARMEHUTU (Party for the Emancipation of the Hutu people) 'was a curious mix of racial enfranchisement, social justice, the extension of economic privileges and anti-communism'.[28] The Belgians, after backing the Tutsis for decades, decided that the easiest route to protect their economic interests was to back PARMEHUTU. Their resolve was intensified by a series of Hutu led farm workers' revolts in 1959. The departing colonialists now wanted elite Hutus in power in order to hold down the majority of Hutus.

In 1959 open fighting began and Belgian paratroopers fought side by side with Hutu militias to oust Tutsi rule. The Belgians also replaced Tutsi chiefs with Hutus, leading to persecution of poor Tutsis by rich Hutus. Over 125,000 refugees fled to neighbouring countries. Local elections in 1960 saw PARMEHUTU win two thirds of the seats and it took 78 percent of the votes in legislative elections a year later. The Hutu elite had taken charge.

This process is known as the '1959 Revolution'; in reality it was simply the replacement of one elite by another, and with the help of the colonial power and the Catholic church. There was no significant land reform—the peasants remained peasants who did not own their land. Only their landlords changed.[29] The new Rwanda was an incredibly conservative country. While socialism and revolution were discussed in much of Africa, Rwanda's leaders were celebrated by Tories in Europe, particularly in Belgium.

The government's only basis of support was to play the ethnic card. Tutsis were 9 percent of the population, said President Kayibanda, so they should not have more than 9 percent of schoolchildren, teachers, etc. This policy caused huge suffering for the Tutsis without in any way helping the vast majority of Hutus.

Throughout the 1960s Tutsi exiles formed guerilla bands and attacked from Zaire, Uganda, Burundi and Tanzania. They were always soundly beaten by an army that was still led by Belgians and could call on Belgian troops in time of need. In 1963 Hutu gangs killed an estimated 10,000 Tutsis while the government executed prominent Tutsi leaders. Another round of killing followed in 1967 and the UN commission of inquiry found the rural areas 'in a state of high tension, a barely suppressed collective panic'.[30]

By 1972 the Kayibanda regime was politically and economically bankrupt. In a desperate effort to survive, the government called for yet another programme of 'purification' to drive the Tutsis from schools, universities, the civil service and even private business. The regime believed this would strike a chord in the wake of the butchery of Hutus by the Tutsi led army in Burundi. The call for ethnic cleansing was taken up most eagerly by richer Hutus who hoped to gain by driving out their Tutsi business and professional rivals. But in the countryside the campaign was virtually ignored. Few people were killed during the crusade, but another vast wave of Tutsi migration followed.

However, the government's strategy backfired. The Hutu vigilante committees, set up to attack the Tutsis, split on regional lines. Peasants even started to fight their landlords—and to settle grievances without considering ethnicity. This was much closer to the prospect of real revolution than anything that occurred in 1959-61. It was extremely dangerous for the rich and in 1973 Major-General Juvenal Habyarimana took power in a coup. He was pledged to give new impetus to Rwanda's development and justice for all.

Independence and new rulers—Burundi

The end of colonialism was clearly going to be extremely destabilising. In Burundi the main challenge to Belgian rule was UPRONA (Union for National Progress) led by the very popular Prince Louis Rwagasore. The colonialists feared UPRONA which they saw as radical and anti-Belgian, dangerously similar to the movement around Lumumba in the Congo. So the Belgians backed the rival PDC (Christian Democrat Party) with money and resources while imposing crippling restrictions on UPRONA.

The UPRONA-PDC rivalry was not a Hutu-Tutsi split. Both parties were led by groups based on different sections of the princely caste. They appealed to people on a political basis—UPRONA was for kicking the Belgians out and reform, PDC for working alongside the Belgians for a long time. When full elections were finally held in September 1961, UPRONA won spectacularly with 58 seats out of 64. Rwagasore became prime minister but was assassinated by a Greek gunman hired by the

PDC supported by the Belgian authorities.[31] The murder led to the crystallisation of ethnic tensions and triggered a bitter struggle for the leadership of UPRONA between Hutu and Tutsi elites.[32]

The details of this process are carefully described in Réne Lemonchard's book, although he overstates ideological factors and underplays material questions. He does show powerfully that after 1961 both group elites turned away from 'national development' and instead sought support by embracing ethnic politics. Tutsi elites gradually used the privileges they had won under colonialism to entrench themselves in the new state. By 1964 they held 83 of the top 133 high ranking civil service posts.[33] Even trade unions and student organisations were also split between Hutu and Tutsi groups. Most crucially, the Tutsi elite held control of the army, which was to prove very important as elections became secondary to guns in determining who would govern.

Developing tensions reached fever pitch in January 1965 when Burundi's president, Pierre Ngendandumwe (a Hutu), was assassinated. Elections a few months later returned a Hutu majority (23 out of 33 seats) in the national assembly. But the king refused to appoint a Hutu prime minister. In response a group of Hutu army officers shot the new prime minister and Hutu troops revolted against the Tutsi officers. The ensuing Tutsi purge led to 'the physical elimination of the entire first generation of Hutu leaders'.[34] General Michel Micombero, a Tutsi army leader, proclaimed Burundi a republic under the slogan of 'Unity and revolution'. Rarely has a declared theme been so false. Micombero accelerated the purges of Hutus from the army and the state and he consolidated the hold of the Tutsi elite over the country's economy.

In 1972 a rebellion by Hutus broke out in the Imbo plain region. There was some organisation in advance, but it was certainly not the national uprising backed by foreign powers that Micombero alleged. In the first phase of the revolt some thousands of Tutsis were killed. But, just as in 1965, the repression was out of all proportion. Estimates of the number of Hutus killed range from 100,000 to 300,000. 'The carnage continued until almost every educated Hutu was either dead or in exile'.[35] Part of the motivation for the killings was economic.[36] The result was that:

For the next 15 years, only Tutsi were qualified to gain access to power, influence and wealth. To an even greater extent than before, what was left of Hutu society was systematically excluded from the army, the civil service and the university.[37]

It is very important to note that, just as in Rwanda 20 years later, there was opposition from members of all groups to the slaughter. The US deputy chief of mission cabled home, 'We have reliable reports that some

Tutsis urging restraint on the basis that the situation has gone too far are being arrested and immediately executed'.[38] This Tutsi heroism contrasted sharply with the attitude of foreign powers. The US ambassador was brazen—'The United States simply should not interfere in any way with the internal affairs of another country',[39] he declared as the body count rose.

The 1972 killing meant the Tutsi elite were firmly established, but they were not a wholly united group.[40] In November 1976 Lieutenant-Colonel Jean-Baptiste Bagaza took power in a bloodless coup. Bagaza was keen on rhetoric which stressed national unity and the struggle against 'the reactionary bourgeoisie, which stands as the principal enemy of our struggle'.[41] He instituted very limited land reform and allowed the formation of trade unions. But Tutsis still controlled every aspect of society and government sponsored repression continued.

As economic crisis came in 1986, it had the same destabilising effect as it did in Rwanda. Bagaza responded by forcing though a range of cuts, but undermined his own authority by attempting to to cut spending on the army. In September 1987 Bagaza was deposed by a coup led by Major Pierre Buyoya. In the middle of 1988 a revolt by Hutus prompted the familiar terrible retaliation from the Tutsi led army. There were massacres by both sides, although the army's were much worse.

In 1972 the rest of the world had ignored the killings: in 1988 the West told Buyoya that he must prevent the continuation of the ethnic hatreds. He appointed a Hutu as prime minister and added Hutus to his cabinet. By the end of 1990 politics and the civil service had been opened up to Hutus. However, the make up of the army hardly altered at all. Coup attempts in February 1989 and March 1992, rather reluctantly put down by the army, reminded Buyoya that he had better not go too far.

In elections in June 1993 Melchior Ndadaye, a Hutu, won almost two thirds of the vote. In what appeared a remarkably democratic response to the result, Buyoya immediately admitted defeat, called for calm, embraced his successor and stepped down. However, the Tutsi elite refused to be displaced without a struggle. Ndadaye's task was made the more difficult by his decision to implement the IMF's Structural Adjustment Programme, which led to price rises for basic goods, devaluation and privatisation. The mass of peasants saw that democracy was combined with a harsh austerity programme. Disillusion with the regime made mass risings in its defence less likely.

In October 1993 the army removed Ndadaye from office. Some Hutus rose to defend the elected government. The army responded in its 'normal' murderous way. Up to 50,000 people died, roughly the same number of Hutus and Tutsis. About 700,000 people, mainly Hutu, fled to neighbouring countries. Almost half a million went to Rwanda where they provided ready recruits for the militias.

The Burundi coup left the country in anarchy. By June this year the number of killings had reached 1,000 a month at least. In July 1996 the Hutu president Sylvestre Ntibantunganya was overthrown and Pierre Buyoya returned once more to take power. After losing the election in 1993, he benefited from a great deal of US funding designed to encourage 'moderates'. Buyoya's return led to widespread sanctions against Burundi (including by the US—against their own protege), which continue as this article goes to press.

The violence in Burundi is not some unfathomable blood feud based on tribalism. It flows from the way divisions were developed by colonialism and then further institutionalised by the post-colonial governments. Economic crisis has made scapegoating by the ruling class more effective. The domination of politics by elites of both groups has made it hard for an alternative to emerge which could appeal to all of the poor against all of the rich. Appeals for unity must be framed in terms of throwing off the fearful conditions that all the exploited and oppressed face, not simply in terms of 'fairness'.

Countdown to the present—Rwanda

Major General Habyarimana's ascent to power in 1973 was generally welcomed. He seemed 'cleaner' than his predecessors. Discrimination against the Tutsis continued. 'Throughout the Habyarimana years there was only one Tutsi officer in the whole army, two Tutsi MPs out of 70 and only one Tutsi cabinet minister out of 30 members'.[42] However, despite the discrimination the Tutsi rich could prosper and were content.[43] Class tensions were held down.

There was very little democracy. Every Rwandese citizen had to join Habyarimana's MRND movement. The president was triumphantly re-elected twice (as sole candidate), once with of 99.98 of the vote and, in a closer contest, with only 99.96 percent. Habyarimana's government was described by one of his European fans as a 'development dictatorship'.[44] Public works such as irrigation, drainage ditches and school building were carried out through the use of forced labour. These work parties, known as the *interahamwe*, would later become death squads.

But from 1973 to about 1990, Rwanda was relatively peaceful. This had little to do with Habyarimana himself and much to do with the generally stable price of coffee and tin. The economic blizzard of the later 1980s caused havoc. The striped blazer brigade on the London commodity exchange traded Rwanda's coffee and tin. As they settled the claims of supply and demand, matched the purchasing power of the multinationals against the weakness of African countries, they were sealing the fate of peasants 6,000 miles away. Gérard Prunier, writes:

> *The political stability of the regime followed almost exactly the curve of*
> *coffee and tin prices. For the elite of the regime there were three sources of*
> *enrichment: coffee and tea exports, briefly tin exports and creaming off*
> *foreign aid. Since a fair share of the first two had to be allocated to running*
> *the government, by 1988 the shrinking sources of revenue left only the third*
> *as a viable alternative. There was an increase in competition for access to*
> *this very specialised resource. The various gentlemen's agreements which*
> *had existed between the competing political clans started to melt down as the*
> *resources shrank and internal power struggles intensified.*[45]

Internal battles meant not only further pressure on the Tutsi elite, but also more clashes between regional leaders who were Hutu. These battles were projected onto the much bigger screen of the tensions created over a century by colonialism and its aftermath. The countdown to murder had begun.

In 1989 the government budget was cut by 40 percent. The peasantry faced huge increases in water fees, health charges, school fees, etc. Land became scarce as farmers tried to increase their holdings to make up for the fall in raw material prices.[46] The peasantry (both Hutu and Tutsi) were on the verge of open rebellion by 1990. The state absorbed more and more of the land which parents hoped to pass on to their children. State tea plantations opened up new sources of foreign exchange but restricted family holdings. The IMF's structural adjustment programme for Rwanda was imposed in 1990. As usual it meant the removal of food subsidies, privatisation and devaluation—and job losses.[47]

The World Bank and the IMF took no account of the likely effects of their shock therapy on a country that was ripe for civil war and had a history of massacres:

> *A second devaluation followed in June 1992. Just as the war began, these*
> [economic changes] *saw urban living standards cut and a dramatic decline in*
> *the standards of health care and education. Inflation accelerated... By 1993,*
> *there was acute hunger in much of southern Rwanda.*[48]

Habyarimana's moves towards multi-partyism after 1990 paradoxically also increased the tension. The elites prepared for a new round of power battles while the state employees anticipated more job cuts if their patron was ousted. In Rwanda:

> *the government used its well-established technique of scapegoating. The*
> *grievances of the rural Hutu population were redirected to the Tutsi minority.*[49]

This process was made much easier by the lack of a political force which offered a class fight of poor against rich rather than Hutus against Tutsis. The Hutu opposition politicians were almost all smeared with participation in elite politics. Nobody believed they were after anything but their own interests.

Those who fled faced a grim future. In Burundi, although the Tutsis continued to run the state machine, the Rwandese Tutsis faced discrimination at every level and were never fully accepted. In Zaire the dictator, Mobutu, was very close to Habyarimana and had no time for his opponents. Tanzania was the least hostile and offered citizenship which many refugees took, but they were still discriminated against. In Uganda many refugees became integrated into the local society, but they were then scapegoated by Ugandan president Milton Obote in the early 1980s as he sought a target to deflect attention from his own problems. This convinced many refugees of the need to return to Rwanda, and increased their willingness to work with Ugandan opposition politicians. Many joined the National Resistance Army of Yoweri Museveni, which succeeded in overthrowing Obote in 1986.

The Rwandese Patriotic Front (RPF), originally formed by refugees from the 1959-1967 wave of killings, thus had a secure base to launch military raids against Habyarimana, but it was incapable of making an appeal to the Hutu masses. The RPF also 'counted among its members a considerable number of Tutsi supremacists for whom the Hutu were a despicable and backward mass of peasants'.[50] It was therefore quite easy for Habyarimana to paint the RPF as simply dedicated to restoring Tutsi dominance.

In October 1990 elements of the RPF tried to invade from Uganda but the attack was beaten back with heavy losses. Partly this was because the French (Socialist Party) government gave Habyarimana full support, despite his human rights defects. In 1990 troops were sent to 'protect French nationals'—in reality they helped the Rwandese government beat the RPF. 'This blind commitment was to have catastrophic consequences because, as the situation radicalised, the Rwandese leadership kept believing that no matter what it did French support would be forthcoming'.[51] The French intervention throughout was like 'giving brandy bottles to an alcoholic', says Prunier.[52]

The defeat of the RPF did not solve Habyarimana's problems; in February 1993 the RPF launched a very serious attack that reached the outskirts of the capital, Kigali. It was halted only by the intervention of French troops. Habyarimana was forced to sign an agreement ('The Arusha Accords') providing for a transitional government and elections.

Had the elections gone ahead, the Habyarimana regime was very unlikely to have survived. It therefore faced a deep crisis. Habyarimana himself might not have contemplated genocide as a 'scapegoating' way out, but he had created a machine which was quite ready for such work, and had been preparing for it for some time. Killing a million people requires organisation. Since the RPF incursions of 1990, a whole set up of roadblocks, gendarmerie and local militias (the *interahamwe*) had been created. These were honed in a series of massacres during 1991 and 1992. Mass killing also requires the efficient targeting of victims. The system of identity cards, which had been rigidly kept and updated, made it easy for Tutsis to be selected.

Throughout 1993 more and more of the population were armed. Many of the arms were 'low-tech weapons' like machetes, studded clubs, knives and spears. A large number of machetes were imported from China in the years before the 1994 killings. But more advanced weapons were also important.[53] The major arms suppliers to the Rwandese government were France, Egypt and South Africa. Before 1990 Belgium was a leading supplier. In 1991-1992 France supplied at least 6 million dollars worth of equipment, training and 700 troops up to 1993. President Habyarimana was supplied with a personal plane by Jean-Christophe Mitterrand, the son of the French president.

Habyarimana was also being pushed by international pressure to allow reform. In April 1994 he flew to Tanzania and, much against his will, was persuaded by neighbouring governments to pledge almost immediate implementation of the Arusha Accords. On the next evening his plane was shot down as it neared Kigali airport and Habyarimana was killed. The government blamed the RPF, or the Belgians, or even the United Nations. Most commentators believe that Hutu extremists, who had of course been encouraged by Habyarimana for decades, were responsible. They had turned on the president for 'selling out'.

Whoever fired the crucial missile, Habyarimana's death was the signal for the killing to begin. In the next three months around 1 million people died.

Did everyone take part?

In one respect the Rwandan slaughter seems to be even worse than the Holocaust. The Nazis' murder of the Jews was (despite recent efforts to prove the contrary) carried out by a tiny minority of the population, almost all of them state functionaries. The reverse was apparently true in Rwanda. Fergal Keane describes the April 1994 killings as 'a crime of mass complicity' in which the educated elite shared with the ragged peasants and the soldiers the fact that 'they were drowning in the blood of their fellow countrymen'.[54]

Radio stations called for genocide; on 6 April 1994 *Radio Télévision*

Libres des Milles Collines,

> told the Hutu population 'the Tutsis need to be killed'. It called on people to 'hunt out the Tutsi'. It asked Rwandans 'the grave is half-empty, who will help to fill it?'[55]

An earlier programme had featured the president of the radio station, Felien Kabuga. He reminded his listeners of the myth that Tutsis had originated in Ethiopia and urged them to 'send the Tutsi home by the rivers'.[56] Radio Rwanda, the equivalent of our BBC, was even more disastrously effective. An opposition journalist says:

> Radio Rwanda was more veiled and ambiguous. But of course all Rwandans knew the message. They would make statements like, 'The enemy—we know him. We only have one enemy; it is he who has never accepted the fact of the republic. The majority of the population, rise up and make sure that the enemy and his accomplices are not around you'.[57]

Many ordinary people ended up taking part in the killings. But immense intimidation, terror and pressure was used by the small core of dedicated murderers to achieve this. Those who initiated the bloodshed wanted to create 'a community of murderers' so that all were implicated. The first targets of the killers on 6 April were not Tutsis but opposition Hutus.

> In the first two days of the killing, the great majority of victims were prominent politicians, senior civil servants, wealthy businessmen with ties to the political opposition, critical journalists and human rights activists. Most were Hutu.[58]

The intention was to physically remove the threat of Hutus resisting the butchery.

All the leading figures of the opposition parties were wiped out, except for the cases where they embraced the carnage. When state officials (mostly Hutus) or civil servants were regarded as suspect or refused to organise slaughter, they were themselves killed. Jean-Baptiste Habyarimana,[59] the prefect of Butare, was opposed to unleashing the killers in his area. He was removed and subsequently killed, together with his family.

Journalists were also early targets. The regime had repressed dissent for years but after 6 April 'censorship and harassment took their ultimate form: mass murder'.[60] Human rights activists and lawyers were also hunted. Hundreds of those in 'subversive' groups like the Association of

Peace Volunteers and the Christian League for the Defence of Human Rights in Rwanda were killed. Their views had to be smashed. It is essential to emphasise that even after the killing had become widespread:

> *Under the most difficult and dangerous circumstances imaginable, many*
> *ordinary Rwandese did their utmost to resist the genocidal slaughter...*
> *Throughout the country ordinary Hutu people concealed Tutsi. They knew*
> *that the price of being discovered was probably death.*[61]

The penalties for those who aided Tutsis were indeed barbaric. Boniface Ndekezi, a peasant from Gitarama, recalls:

> *The **interahamwe** came to search our house. They found a Tutsi my father*
> *had hidden. They not only killed the Tutsi, they also killed seven members of*
> *our family, my father, my brother and five sisters. They killed everybody they*
> *found in the house.*[62]

Even the slightest respect to Tutsis could lead to death.[63]

There was also an important class element. 'Among a wide range of Tutsis there was a consensus that uneducated farmers were far more helpful and courageous than those "who sat in offices and understood the politics at hand"'.[64] It is the great strength of the African Rights book that it insists on the way in which ordinary people frequently reacted against the massacres and only took part after the most ferocious pressure. Fergal Keane seems much less aware of this critical point. In contrast to the heroism of peasants, the hundreds of French and Belgian troops were ordered by their governments not to stand in the way of genocide. As mass killing began, some Tutsis were slaughtered under the eyes of the French or Belgian soldiers, who did not react. The French embassy's Tutsi personnel were abandoned to certain death. Leading figures of the Habyarimana regime were welcomed into sanctuary by the French authorities. Ordinary people clinging to the gates were pushed back by the gendarmes.

The killings continued for three months before France again decided to intervene. In June Mitterrand launched Operation Turquoise, stressing 'humanitarian motives'. A powerful armada was sent—2,500 men with more than 100 armoured vehicles, artillery batteries, ten helicopters and jets for air cover. The force was hugely welcomed by the retreating government forces which by this time were on the verge of total defeat by the RPF. Prunier writes that enormous French tricolours were displayed everywhere on government vehicles:

> *They proved to be an embarrassment, not only because of the press, but*

because, on seeing French flags, hidden Tutsi would come out of hiding only to be immediately killed by the soldiers of the militiamen. As a French solider protested, 'I am fed up with being cheered along by murderers'.[65]

An eyewitness in Kigali in 1994 says it was common to hear the French president called 'Mitterahamwe'. The sole effect of the French force was to protect some of the most bestial organisers of the genocide.

The killings stopped after the victory of the RPF forces, which had invaded as soon as the massacres began. Almost everyone who had been targeted was either dead, had fled or was in hiding. As the RPF swept to victory, another vast human tragedy unfolded. Millions of refugees moved into neighbouring countries, encouraged by the Hutu leaders to believe they would be massacred if they stayed. The RPF took over a country large parts of which were deserted.

The West made conditions especially hard for the new government in Rwanda. New loans were available, once the old ones had been cleared, so, for example, £100 million of World Bank money was held back because £3 million had not been paid by Habyarimana.[66] The new regime was initially a mixed Hutu-Tutsi administration, but last year several Hutus resigned or were sacked. Ostensibly in the search for those who led the genocide, 80,000 people have been locked up; nobody has yet been brought to trial. *The Economist* reports:

In one town, Cyangugu, all the Hutus were recently rounded up and forced to stand in a stadium without food or water until they identified the killers among them. Beneath its veneer does the RPF stand for Tutsi survival—or for Tutsi domination?[67]

Waiting for the next massacre

This tragedy has resulted from the development of capitalism, but capitalism itself has no answers to it. Perhaps if there was a sustained upturn in the world economy then the pressure towards violence might be lessened, but there is no sign of such an upturn and, if it comes, it is unlikely to last long. International capital has virtually abandoned any interest in Rwanda and Burundi. The death of a million in Rwanda did not cause the slightest tremor to the stock markets. Reformism also offers nothing. Even had the rulers of Rwanda and Burundi had noble motives (and they did not) they would have been broken by the markets, the demands of the IMF and the collapse of coffee and tin prices in 1986. The only hope for Rwanda and Burundi lies in developing the unity of ordinary people which has survived even in the most hostile conditions and despite the immense pressure from the top against it.

The only way that the unity will be realised is through common struggle in order to improve the lot of all the poor whatever identity card they carry, by battling against the rich, whatever group they come from. That will have to be a revolutionary fight. It is hard to see such an alternative emerging in the near future. Perhaps it will take the example of successful struggle by workers in Nigeria or South Africa or Zimbabwe to give it real impetus. Rosa Luxemburg's account of the choice facing the world between socialism or barbarism is no longer a prediction. It is reality today in central Africa. Capitalism has indeed produced barbarism. Only workers' struggle could end it.

Notes

1 F Keane, *Season of Blood, a Rwandan Journey* (Penguin, 1996), p29.

2 R Lemarchand, *Burundi: Ethnic Conflict and Genocide* (Cambridge University Press, 1996), pxxv.

3 As I wrote this article in the middle of October 1996, there were reports of fighting in eastern Zaire. The key elements in the conflict are the attempt by President Mobutu to deflect attention from his own problems and his theft of a country's wealth by refusing to grant 'foreigners' citizenship and playing them off against other locals; Mobutu's aid to the Hutu militia leaders who fled Rwanda in 1994; the hundreds of thousands of Rwandese refugees who remain in terrible conditions in refugee camps in Zaire and are bitter at their suffering over the last two years; the willingness of the Rwandese and Burundian governments to arm their Tutsi supporters in Kivu; the desperation of all ordinary people in the area who feel on the brink of starvation and in competition with each other. The UN special rapporteur on human rights in Zaire spoke recently of 'government sponsored massacres'. The UN also claims that several murderous militias have already committed terrible crimes. See, for example, *The Economist*, 19 October 1996.

4 There is a fierce debate about practically all the elements I describe here. For example, W Rodney in *How Europe Underdeveloped Africa* (Dar-es-Salam 1971), D Newbury in *The Invention of Rwanda: The Alchemy of Ethnicity* (University of North Carolina, 1995). There is a good discussion of these issues in M Mamdani, "From Conquest to Consent as the Basis of State Formation: Reflections on Rwanda', *New Left Review* 216.

5 African Rights, *Rwanda: Death, Despair and Defiance* (London, 1995), p3.

6 Ibid.

7 G Prunier, *The Rwanda Crisis: History of a Genocide* (London, 1995), p19.

8 Ibid, p15.

9 Ibid, p3.

10 F Reyntjens, *Burundi: Breaking the Cycle of Violence* (Minority Rights Group, 1995), p7.

11 P Gourevitch, 'The Poisoned Country', *The New York Review of Books*, 6 June 1996.

12 F Reyntjens, op cit, p7.

13 African Rights, op cit, p5.

14 M Mamdani, op cit, p5.

15 African Rights, op cit, p648.

16 G Prunier, op cit, p25:'Thus from the start the European presence was a determining factor in reinforcing the mwamiship, the chiefly hierarchy and the court's increasing hold over the lightly-controlled peripheral areas'.

17   Ibid.
18   Ibid, p26.
19   Ibid.
20   Ibid, p6.
21   Ibid.
22   Ibid, p8.
23   Ibid, p27.
24   Ibid, p35.
25   Ibid, p50.
26   Ibid, pp38-39.
27   Ibid, p39.
28   African Rights, op cit, p11.
29   African Rights, op cit, pp11-12.
30   Ibid, p13.
31   R Lemarchand, op cit, p55.
32   Ibid, p59.
33   Ibid, p66.
34   Ibid, p72.
35   Ibid, p97.
36   Ibid, p102.
37   Ibid, p103.
38   Ibid, p97.
39   Ibid, p130.
40   Ibid, p107.
41   Ibid.
42   G Prunier, op cit, p75.
43   Ibid, p76.
44   Ibid, p77.
45   Ibid, p84.
46   Ibid, p88.
47   African Rights, op cit, p20: 'The structural adjustment programme not only
      choked off any possibility of new recruitment into the bureaucratic pyramid, but
      threatened the jobs of those who were already there. Low ranking officials in the
      villages—including administrators, teachers, agricultural extension workers,
      health workers and policemen—saw their prospects of promotion vanish, and
      even faced the possibility of losing their jobs altogether.'
48   Ibid.
49   Ibid, p24.
50   G Prunier, op cit, p151.
51   Ibid, p107.
52   Ibid, p352.
53   Guns were quite scarce in 1994. Victims were sometimes offered the choice of
      being chopped to death or paying a large sum to be shot.
54   F Keane, op cit, p29.
55   African Rights, op cit, p80.
56   Ibid, p79.
57   Ibid, p85.
58   Ibid, p178.
59   This Habyarimana was no relative of the country's leader. In Rwanda and Burundi
      parents choose surnames for the children as well as first names, so people are
      often named after leading figures.
60   African Rights, op cit, p201.
61   Ibid, pxxvii/xxviii
62   Ibid, p1017.

63   Ibid, p1022.
64   Ibid, p1024.
65   G Prunier, op cit, p292. Given how clear Prunier is about the French invasion, it is
      remarkable that in November 1996 he saw French intervention as the only way
      forward in eastern Zaire.
66   Ibid, p336.
67   *The Economist,* 19 October 1996.

The Socialist Workers Party is one of an international grouping of socialist organisations:

AUSTRALIA: International Socialists, PO Box A338, Sydney South

BELGIUM: Socialisme International, Rue Lovinfosse 60, 4030 Grivengée

BRITAIN: Socialist Workers Party, PO Box 82, London E3

CANADA: International Socialists, PO Box 339, Station E, Toronto, Ontario M6H 4E3

CYPRUS: Ergatiki Demokratia, PO Box 7280, Nicosia

DENMARK: Internationale Socialister, Postboks 642, 2200 København N

FRANCE: Socialisme International, BP 189, 75926 Paris Cedex 19

GREECE: Organosi Sosialisliki Epanastasi, c/o Workers Solidarity, PO Box 8161, Athens 100 10

HOLLAND: International Socialists, PO Box 9720, 3506 GR Utrecht

IRELAND: Socialist Workers Party, PO Box 1648, Dublin 8

NORWAY: Internasjonale Socialisterr, Postboks 5370, Majorstua, 0304 Oslo 3

POLAND: Solidarność Socjalistyczna, PO Box 12, 01-900 Warszawa 118

SOUTH AFRICA: Socialist Workers Organisation, PO Box 18530, Hillbrow 2038, Johannesburg

SPAIN: Socialismo International, Apartardo 563, 08080, Barcelona

UNITED STATES: International Socialist Organisation, PO Box 16085, Chicago, Illinois 60616

ZIMBABWE: International Socialist Organisation, PO Box 6758, Harare

The following issues of *International Socialism* (second series) are available price £3 (including postage) from IS Journal, PO Box 82, London E3 3LH. *International Socialism* 2:58 and 2:65 are available on cassette from the Royal National Institute for the Blind (Peterborough Library Unit). Phone 01733 370777.

International Socialism 2:72 Autumn 1996
Alex Callinicos: Betrayal and discontent: Labour under Blair ★ Sue Cockerill and Colin Sparks: Japan in crisis ★ Richard Levins: When science fails us ★ Ian Birchall: The Babeuf bicentenary: conspiracy or revolutionary party? ★ Brian Manning: A voice for the poor ★ Paul O'Flinn: From the kingdom of necessity to the kingdom of freedom: Morris's *News from Nowhere* ★ Clare Fermont: Bookwatch: Palestine and the Middle East 'peace process'★

International Socialism 2:71 Summer 1996
Chris Harman: The crisis of bourgeois economics ★ Hassan Mahamdallie: William Morris and revolutionary Marxism ★ Alex Callinicos: Darwin, materialism and revolution ★ Chris Nineham: Raymond Williams: revitalising the left? ★ Paul Foot: A passionate prophet of liberation ★ Gill Hubbard: Why has feminism failed women? ★ Lee Sustar: Bookwatch: fighting to unite black and white★

International Socialism 2:70 Spring 1996
Alex Callinicos: South Africa after apartheid ★ Chris Harman: France's hot December ★ Brian Richardson: The making of a revolutionary ★ Gareth Jenkins: Why Lucky Jim turned right—an obituary of Kingsley Amis ★ Mark O'Brien: The bloody birth of capitalism ★ Lee Humber: Studies in revolution ★ Adrian Budd: A new life for Lenin ★ Martin Smith: Bookwatch: the General Strike★

International Socialism 2:69 Winter 1995
Lindsey German: The Balkan war: can there be peace? ★ Duncan Blackie: The left and the Balkan war ★ Nicolai Gentchev: The myth of welfare dependency ★ Judy Cox: Wealth, poverty and class in Britain today ★ Peter Morgan: Trade unions and strikes ★ Julie Waterson: The party at its peak ★ Megan Trudell: Living to some purpose ★ Nick Howard: The rise and fall of socialism in one city ★ Andy Durgan: Bookwatch: Civil war and revolution in Spain ★

International Socialism 2:68 Autumn 1995
Ruth Brown: Racism and immigration in Britain ★ John Molyneux: Is Marxism deterministic? ★ Stuart Hood: News from nowhere? ★ Lee Sustar: Communism in the heart of the beast ★ Peter Linebaugh: To the teeth and forehead of our faults ★ George Paizis: Back to the future ★ Phil Marshall: The children of stalinism ★ Paul D'Amato: Bookwatch: 100 years of cinema ★

International Socialism 2:67 Summer 1995
Paul Foot: When will the Blair bubble burst? ★ Chris Harman: From Bernstein to Blair—100 years of revisionism ★ Chris Bambery: Was the Second World War a war for democracy? ★ Chris Nineham: Is the media all powerful? ★ Peter Morgan: How the West was won ★ Charlie Hore: Bookwatch: China since Mao ★

International Socialism 2:66 Spring 1995
Dave Crouch: The crisis in Russia and the rise of the right ★ Phil Gasper: Cruel and unusual punishment: the politics of crime in the United States ★ Alex Callinicos: Backwards to liberalism ★ John Newsinger: Matewan: film and working class struggle ★ John Rees: The light and the dark ★ Judy Cox: How to make the Tories disappear ★ Charlie Hore: Jazz: a reply to the critics ★ Pat Riordan: Bookwatch: Ireland ★

International Socialism 2:65 Special issue
Lindsey German: Frederick Engels: life of a revolutionary ★ John Rees: Engels' Marxism ★ Chris Harman: Engels and the origins of human society ★ Paul McGarr: Engels and natural science ★

International Socialism 2:64 Autumn 1994
Chris Harman: The prophet and the proletariat ★ Kieran Allen: What is changing in Ireland ★ Mike Haynes: The wrong road on Russia ★ Rob Ferguson: Hero and villain ★ Jane Elderton: Suffragette style ★ Chris Nineham: Two faces of modernism ★ Mike Hobart, Dave Harker and Matt

Kelly: Three replies to 'Jazz—a people's music?' ★ Charlie Kimber: Bookwatch: South Africa—the struggle continues ★

International Socialism 2:63 Summer 1994
Alex Callinicos: Crisis and class struggle in Europe today ★ Duncan Blackie: The United Nations and the politics of imperialism ★ Brian Manning: The English Revolution and the transition from feudalism to capitalism ★ Lee Sustar: The roots of multi-racial labour unity in the United States ★ Peter Linebaugh: Days of villainy: a reply to two critics ★ Dave Sherry: Trotsky's last, greatest struggle ★ Peter Morgan: Geronimo and the end of the Indian wars ★ Dave Beecham: Ignazio Silone and *Fontamara* ★ Chris Bambery: Bookwatch: understanding fascism ★

International Socialism 2:62 Spring 1994
Sharon Smith: Mistaken identity—or can identity politics liberate the oppressed? ★ Iain Ferguson: Containing the crisis—crime and the Tories ★ John Newsinger: Orwell and the Spanish Revolution ★ Chris Harman: Change at the first millenium ★ Adrian Budd: Nation and empire—Labour's foreign policy 1945-51 ★ Gareth Jenkins: Novel questions ★ Judy Cox: Blake's revolution ★ Derek Howl: Bookwatch: the Russian Revolution ★

International Socialism 2:61 Winter 1994
Lindsey German: Before the flood? ★ John Molyneux: The 'politically correct' controversy ★ David McNally: E P Thompson—class struggle and historical materialism ★ Charlie Hore: Jazz—a people's music ★ Donny Gluckstein: Revolution and the challenge of labour ★ Charlie Kimber: Bookwatch: the Labour Party in decline ★

International Socialism 2:60 Autumn 1993
Chris Bambery: Euro-fascism: the lessons of the past and present tasks ★ Chris Harman: Where is capitalism going? (part 2) ★ Mike Gonzalez: Chile and the struggle for workers' power ★ Phil Marshall: Bookwatch: Islamic activism in the Middle East ★

International Socialism 2:59 Summer 1993
Ann Rogers: Back to the workhouse ★ Kevin Corr and Andy Brown: The labour aristocracy and the roots of reformism ★ Brian Manning: God, Hill and Marx ★ Henry Maitles: Cutting the wire: a criticial appraisal of Primo Levi ★ Hazel Croft: Bookwatch: women and work ★

International Socialism 2:58 Spring 1993
Chris Harman: Where is capitalism going? (part one) ★ Ruth Brown and Peter Morgan: Politics and the class struggle today: a roundtable discussion ★ Richard Greeman: The return of Comrade Tulayev: Victor Serge and the tragic vision of Stalinism ★ Norah Carlin: A new English revolution ★ John Charlton: Building a new world ★ Colin Barker: A reply to Dave McNally ★

International Socialism 2:57 Winter 1992
Lindsey German: Can there be a revolution in Britain? ★ Mike Haynes: Columbus, the Americas and the rise of capitalism ★ Mike Gonzalez: The myths of Columbus: a history ★ Paul Foot: Poetry and revolution ★ Alex Callinicos: Rhetoric which cannot conceal a bankrupt theory: a reply to Ernest Mandel ★ Charlie Kimber: Capitalism, cruelty and conquest ★ David McNulty: Comments on Colin Barker's review of Thompson's *Customs in Common* ★

International Socialism 2:56 Autumn 1992
Chris Harman: The Return of the National Question ★ Dave Treece: Why the Earth Summit failed ★ Mike Gonzalez: Can Castro survive? ★ Lee Humber and John Rees: The good old cause—an interview with Christopher Hill ★ Ernest Mandel: The Impasse of Schematic Dogmatism ★

International Socialism 2:55 Summer 1992
Alex Callinicos: Race and class ★ Lee Sustar: Racism and class struggle in the American Civil War era ★ Lindsey German and Peter Morgan: Prospects for socialists—an interview with Tony Cliff ★ Robert Service: Did Lenin lead to Stalin? ★ Samuel Farber: In defence of democratic revolutionary socialism ★ David Finkel: Defending 'October' or sectarian dogmatism? ★ Robin Blackburn: Reply to John Rees ★ John Rees: Dedicated followers of fashion ★ Colin Barker: In praise of custom ★ Sheila McGregor: Revolutionary witness ★

International Socialism 2:54 Spring 1992
Sharon Smith: Twilight of the American dream ★ Mike Haynes: Class and crisis—the transition in eastern Europe ★ Costas Kossis: A miracle without end? Japanese capitalism and the world economy ★ Alex Callinicos: Capitalism and the state system: A reply to Nigel Harris ★ Steven Rose: Do animals have rights? ★ John Charlton: Crime and class in the 18th century ★ John Rees: Revolution, reform and working class culture ★ Chris Harman: Blood simple ★

International Socialism 2:52 Autumn 1991
John Rees: In defence of October ★ Ian Taylor and Julie Waterson: The political crisis in Greece—an interview with Maria Styllou and Panos Garganas ★ Paul McGarr: Mozart, overture to revolution ★ Lee Humber: Class, class consciousness and the English Revolution ★ Derek Howl: The legacy of Hal Draper ★

International Socialism 2:51 Summer 1991
Chris Harman: The state and capitalism today ★ Alex Callinicos: The end of nationalism? ★ Sharon Smith: Feminists for a strong state? ★ Colin Sparks and Sue Cockerill: Goodbye to the Swedish miracle ★ Simon Phillips: The South African Communist Party and the South African working class ★ John Brown: Class conflict and the crisis of feudalism ★

International Socialism 2:49 Winter 1990
Chris Bambery: The decline of the Western Communist Parties ★ Ernest Mandel: A theory which has not withstood the test of time ★ Chris Harman: Criticism which does not withstand the test of logic ★ Derek Howl: The law of value In the USSR ★ Terry Eagleton: Shakespeare and the class struggle ★ Lionel Sims: Rape and pre-state societies ★ Sheila McGregor: A reply to Lionel Sims ★

International Socialism 2:48 Autumn 1990
Lindsey German: The last days of Thatcher ★ John Rees: The new imperialism ★ Neil Davidson and Donny Gluckstein: Nationalism and the class struggle in Scotland ★ Paul McGarr: Order out of chaos ★

International Socialism 2:46 Winter 1989
Chris Harman: The storm breaks ★ Alex Callinicos: Can South Africa be reformed? ★ John Saville: Britain, the Marshall Plan and the Cold War ★ Sue Clegg: Against the stream ★ John Rees: The rising bourgeoisie ★

International Socialism 2:44 Autumn 1989
Charlie Hore: China: Tiananmen Square and after ★ Sue Clegg: Thatcher and the welfare state ★ John Molyneux: *Animal Farm* revisited ★ David Finkel: After Arias, is the revolution over? ★ John Rose: Jews in Poland ★

International Socialism 2:43 Summer 1989 (Reprint—special price £4.50)
Marxism and the Great French Revolution by Paul McGarr and Alex Callinicos

International Socialism 2:42 Spring 1989
Chris Harman: The myth of market socialism ★ Norah Carlin: Roots of gay oppression ★ Duncan Blackie: Revolution in science ★ International Socialism Index ★

International Socialism 2:41 Winter 1988
Polish socialists speak out: Solidarity at the Crossroads ★ Mike Haynes: Nightmares of the market ★ Jack Robertson: Socialists and the unions ★ Andy Strouthous: Are the unions in decline? ★ Richard Bradbury: What is Post-Structuralism? ★ Colin Sparks: George Bernard Shaw ★

International Socialism 2:39 Summer 1988
Chris Harman and Andy Zebrowski: Glasnost, before the storm ★ Chanie Rosenberg: Labour and the fight against fascism ★ Mike Gonzalez: Central America after the Peace Plan ★ Ian Birchall: Raymond Williams ★ Alex Callinicos: Reply to John Rees ★

International Socialism 2:35 Summer 1987
Pete Green: Capitalism and the Thatcher years ★ Alex Callinicos: Imperialism, capitalism and the state today ★ Ian Birchall: Five years of *New Socialist* ★ Callinicos and Wood debate 'Looking for alternatives to reformism' ★ David Widgery replies on 'Beating Time' ★

International Socialism 2:31 Winter 1985
Alex Callinicos: Marxism and revolution In South Africa ★ Tony Cliff: The tragedy of A J Cook ★ Nigel Harris: What to do with London? The strategies of the GLC ★

International Socialism 2:30 Autumn 1985
Gareth Jenkins: Where is the Labour Party heading? ★ David McNally: Debt, inflation and the rate of profit ★ Ian Birchall: The terminal crisis in the British Communist Party ★ replies on Women's oppression and *Marxism Today* ★

International Socialism 2:25 Autumn 1984
John Newsinger: Jim Larkin, Syndicalism and the 1913 Dublin Lockout ★ Pete Binns: Revolution and state capitalism in the Third World ★ Colin Sparks: Towards a police state? ★ Dave Lyddon: Demystifying the downturn ★ John Molyneux: Do working class men benefit from women's oppression? ★

International Socialism 2:18 Winter 1983
Donny Gluckstein: Workers' councils in Western Europe ★ Jane Ure Smith: The early Communist press in Britain ★ John Newsinger: The Bolivian Revolution ★ Andy Durgan: Largo Caballero and Spanish socialism ★ M Barker and A Beezer: Scarman and the language of racism ★

International Socialism 2:14 Winter 1981
Chris Harman: The riots of 1981 ★ Dave Beecham: Class struggle under the Tories ★ Tony Cliff: Alexandra Kollontai ★ L James and A Paczuska: Socialism needs feminism ★ reply to Cliff on Zetkin ★ Feminists In the labour movement ★

International Socialism 2:13 Summer 1981
Chris Harman: The crisis last time ★ Tony Cliff: Clara Zetkin ★ Ian Birchall: Left Social Democracy In the French Popular Front ★ Pete Green: Alternative Economic Strategy ★ Tim Potter: The death of Eurocommunism ★

International Socialism 2:12 Spring 1981
Jonathan Neale: The Afghan tragedy ★ Lindsey German: Theories of patriarchy ★ Ray Challinor: McDouall and Physical Force Chartism ★ S Freeman & B Vandesteeg: Unproductive labour ★ Alex Callinicos: Wage labour and capitalism ★ Italian fascism ★ Marx's theory of history ★ Cabral ★